Francoise Darcy-Berube and John Paul Berube

GROWING UP
A FRIEND OF JESUS

A Guide to Discipleship for Children

This book was given

to: _____

by: _____

on: _____

ST. ANTHONY MESSENGER PRESS

Cincinnati, Ohio

NOVALIS

CONTENTS

© 2000 Novalis,
Saint Paul University,
Ottawa, Canada

Published in Canada
by Novalis
Saint Paul University
223 Main Street
Ottawa, Ontario, Canada
K1S 1C4

Published and distributed in
the United States of America
by
St. Anthony Messenger Press
1615 Republic St.
Cincinnati, OH 45210
1-800-488-0488
www.AmericanCatholic.org
ISBN (U.S.) 0-86716-401-8

Canadian Cataloguing in
Publication Data

Darcy-Bérubé, Françoise
Growing up a friend of Jesus:
a guide to discipleship for
children

ISBN 2-89507-041-5

1. Christian life
  –Juvenile literature.
2. Discipling (Christianity)
  –Juvenile literature.
3. Children–Religious life.
I. Bérubé, Jean-Paul
II. Title.

BV4571.2.D37 2000
j248.8'2
C99-901515-X

Printed in Canada.

Imprimatur:
Cardinal Jean-Claude Turcotte,
Archbishop of Montreal,
N.P. 7/1999.

We acknowledge the
financial support of the
Government of Canada
through the Book Publishing
Industry Development
Program (BPIDP) for our
publishing activities.

DESIGN AND LAYOUT:

FLEXIDÉE

ILLUSTRATIONS:

Elsa Myotte
front cover and pages: 4, 5,
8, 9, 12, 13, 14, 15, 26 (Top),
30, 31, 40, 41, 42, 89, 90, 91,
92, 93, 94, 95, 96, 97, 98, 99,
122, 126, 127.

Caroline Mérola
pages: 48, 49, 51, 52, 53, 57,
58, 59, 69, 70, 71.

Monique Chaussé
pages: 20, 21, 34, 35, 36, 37,
44, 45, 54, 55, 56, 62, 63, 64,
65, 76, 77, 78, 79, 80, 81, 82,
83 and mascots Tic and Tac

Anne-Marie Forest
pages: 6, 7, 10, 11, 16, 17,
18, 19, 26 (Bottom), 27 (Top),
28, 29, 32, 33, 38, 39, 43, 46,
47, 60, 61, 66, 67, 68, 84, 85,
86, 87, 88, 106, 107, 108, 109,
112, 113, 114, 115, 116, 117,
118, 119, 122, 123, 128.

Daniela Zékina
pages: 16, 17, 22, 23, 24, 25,
27 (Bottom), 72, 73, 74, 75,
100, 101, 102, 103, 104, 105,
110, 111, 120, 121, 125.

Christine Granger
page: 124.

Dear Parents,

You know better than anyone else how demanding and exhausting the hectic daily routines of your life can be. Little time is left for meaningful conversations with your children, which are so important for their spiritual growth and which they often long for. Even when you do have a little time you may not know where to begin! This book was prepared to offer you lively starting points for such conversations.

Growing Up a Friend of Jesus is not a textbook. It is a handbook, a practical guide to the Christian way of life for children 8 to 11 years old. It is a resource to be consulted often, according to your child's needs. The information which follows will help you and your child use the book efficiently.

It is our heartfelt hope that Growing Up a Friend of Jesus will become for your child and many others a cherished companion-book. May it help them root their life in a truly personal way in our Christian faith and in the love of the Lord. And may that faith and that love help them sail through the approaching rough seas of adolescence more serenely!

AN IMPORTANT STARTING POINT

When your child receives this book, take a few moments to help him or her understand it. The best way to do this is to leaf through the book and the table of contents, then read together pages 7 to 13. This will give you the chance to let your child know that his or her spiritual development is important, and that this book can help on the journey.

- **Part One** gives your child a chance to experience an ongoing initiation into a personal life of prayer. This is a basic requirement for your child's perseverance and growth in faith.

  Even if your family is not used to praying together, even if you are not a practising Christian, as long as you share our Christian faith you can greatly contribute to your child's initiation. You can do this simply by showing genuine interest in what the child is discovering, by encouraging your child to pray each morning and evening, and by sharing occasionally in some of his or her meaningful experiences in prayer.

- While reading the stories and suggestions in **Part Two** of the book, your child will become more aware of his or her own inner self. Your child's questions, fears and hopes, struggles and values, joys and secret pain will rise to the conscious level. This might bring your child very naturally to reflect on his or her life.

  How wonderful it would be if, at such times, you could give your child the opportunity to share these thoughts with you. Listening first is very important. Gently broadening and enriching the reflection is a powerful tool in the moral and spiritual education of your child during these critical years.

- **Part Three** invites your child to take initiative and responsibility to enhance the quality of life and happiness in your family. Those initiatives will, of course, need your support and encouragement if they are to bear fruit.

- **Part Four** provides your child with a variety of prayers for different occasions.

TO YOU, WHOM WE WOULD LOVE TO MEET

Some time ago,
your Christian community
welcomed you with joy
at the Table of the Lord.

It trusted that you were able by now
to start learning on your own
how to live as a friend of Jesus,
how to become a disciple of Jesus.

This book has been written for you
with great love and care,
to help you do just that.
We hope you will enjoy it.

**May you discover more and more
the very special joy we find
when we try to live day by day
as a friend of Jesus.**

Francoise and John Paul

WE ARE PART OF A GREAT STORY

• THE ONE WHO CHANGED EVERYTHING

Some people we meet we soon forget about.
Others change our heart and brighten up
our life forever.

This is what happened to many of the people
who met Jesus in Palestine.
You may already know some of them:
Peter, John, the Samaritan woman,
Martha and Mary, Zacchaeus, the blind man
and many sick people.

When they met Jesus,
their life changed forever.
Many decided right then to listen
to Jesus' call and to follow him.

For more than 2,000 years now, billions of people — women, men and children — have met Jesus in their own way through the faith of the Church. They heard the same call:

BELIEVE IN THE GOOD NEWS. COME, FOLLOW ME!

And from then on, their greatest desire was to join Jesus' followers, to learn to live as his disciples and to work with him to make God's Dream come true.

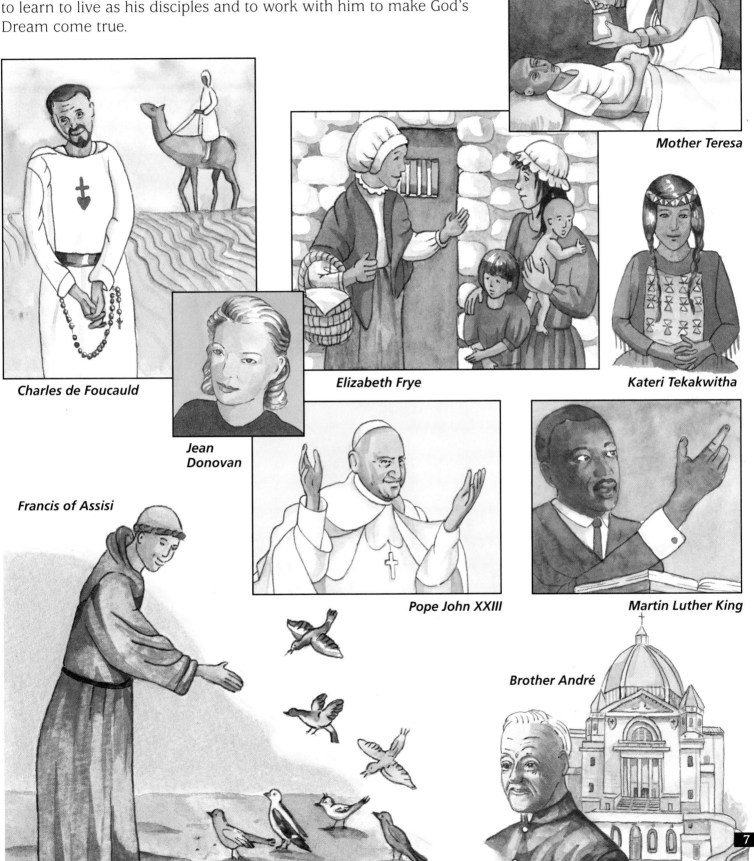

Mother Teresa

Charles de Foucauld

Jean Donovan

Elizabeth Frye

Kateri Tekakwitha

Francis of Assisi

Pope John XXIII

Martin Luther King

Brother André

• TODAY IT IS YOUR TURN...

Because you have been baptized,
because you are part of God's family,
you know that our risen Lord
is calling you and me
and each one of us today:

Believe in the Good News.
Come, follow me.
I am the Light of the world.
If you follow me,
you will not walk in darkness,
but you will have the Light
of eternal life.
(Adapted from Mark and John)

As you already know,
Jesus wants to be your best Friend.
He wants to help you
find the paths to true happiness.
He invites you to join him
in making God's Dream come true.

Following Jesus faithfully
will not always be easy.
Loving as he did
is sometimes quite hard.
You will find that out as you grow up.

But what a great adventure it is
to try building with Jesus,
wherever we are,
a world of justice, love and peace for all!

IF YOU GO AHEAD AND TRUST JESUS,
YOU WILL NEVER REGRET IT.

PART ONE

GROWING IN LOVE WITH GOD THROUGH PRAYER

WHY IS PRAYER SO IMPORTANT IN OUR CHRISTIAN LIFE?

First, because it is our way to express to God our love and our thanks for the gift of our life.

Second, because it is in prayer that we learn day by day to discover and enjoy God's loving presence in our life.

It is that very special joy that Jesus wanted for us when he said: *I want my joy to be in you.* (JOHN 15:11)

A SPECIAL PLACE FOR PRAYER

You know that we can speak to God always and everywhere. But it is helpful to have a special place in your home where you can go when you want to be quiet and pray for a longer while. You could call it a "prayer corner" or a quiet place.

Here are some ideas to help you prepare a beautiful prayer corner in your home.

Jeremy's room is very small, but he found a way to make a lovely prayer corner. He loves the sea and says it's the most wonderful thing God has created.

Emily loves birds and flowers. They make her want to praise God.

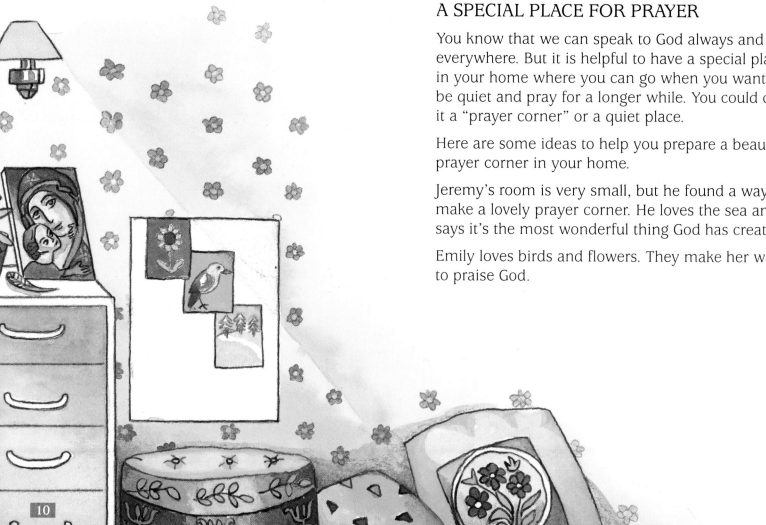

Anything that helps you pray can be put in your prayer corner. Lotus and Xavier prepared their prayer corner together. They wrote down on strips of paper their favourite words of God and put them up. They like to pray together in the evening.

In Dolores' family they like to pray to the saints and have many lovely statues they brought back from Mexico. They pray together every evening.

The Harrison family lives in an old farmhouse. Behind the kitchen there is a small space with a window that looks out on the yard.

The family has decided this would be a quiet place for all to use freely. Whoever is there, reflecting or praying, should not be disturbed. Sometimes they all come there to pray or just be quiet together.

GETTING A GOOD START IN THE MORNING

Each day is a gift.
God invites us to welcome it with joy
and to make something beautiful with it!

On weekdays you don't have time for long prayers: you have to hurry to get ready for school. But you always have time to say "Hi!" to God who gives you this new day. Here is a way to do it:

- First, remember that God is always with you and loves you. To each one of us God says:
  You are precious in my eyes and I love you.
  (ISAIAH 43:4)

- Then pray to God for a brief moment. Here are some short prayers you could learn by heart so you can say or sing one to God before you leave your room or when you are on your way to school. Choose the one that suits your mood of the day.

† *The sun is out,*
  the birds are singing.
  Thank you, God,
  for this new day!

† *Thank you, God,*
  for this new day.
  Help me live it
  in your love.

† *Flowers are thirsty,*
  animals too.
  Blessed be God
  for the rain of today!

† *Praise the Lord*
  who gives us life.
  Praise the Lord
  who loves us all!

† *To you, Lord,*
  I offer the beauty of this day.
  To you, Lord,
  I offer my joy of being alive.

Some days you may feel a little worried when you wake up because you know you will have something hard to do that day. While you are getting ready for the day, tell Jesus about it. Share your worries and ask him to help you. Keep in your heart this word of God: *Don't be afraid. I am always with you.* (ISAIAH 41:10)

† *Lord Jesus, you know*
  it is dark in my heart.
  I am worried and scared.
  Be with me today,
  be my light and my strength,
  keep me walking on your paths.
  Amen.

SPECIAL MORNING PRAYERS
FOR WEEKENDS OR FEAST DAYS

When you don't have to rush to school, you can take a little more time to pray to God.
You might say the *Our Father*, our Christian prayer that Jesus taught us.
Simple gestures may help you pray better.

Our Father

Who art in heaven,

But deliver us from evil.

Lead us not into temptation,

Hallowed be your name,

Remember, millions of Christians around the world pray this prayer every day.

Forgive us our sins as we forgive those who sin against us,

Your Kingdom come,

Give us this day our daily bread,

Your will be done on earth as it is in heaven.

PRAYER OF OFFERING

The next prayer was written especially for people your age. It is a way to offer your life to God our Father with Jesus in thanks. This is what we do in the Eucharist, which is celebrated every day all around the world.

- Stretch your body so that you feel good.
- Then stand straight on both feet. Close your eyes; imagine yourself standing on our beautiful planet Earth.
- Breathe deeply two or three times. Remember that God is looking at you with love. Then pray this way:

Dear God, here I am,

giving thanks for this day.

With Jesus, your Son,

I give you this day,

I give you my love,

and with him I pray:

may your Kingdom come!

ENJOY QUIET TIME IN THE EVENING

Jesus wants to help you become the best person you can be. He wants to lead you to true happiness. But he can only do this if you take the time to listen to him, to learn from him. One of the best times to do that is at night, before bedtime.

- Make yourself comfortable. Breathe deeply a few times.

- Imagine you are with Jesus and his friends in the evening, near the lake. They are all telling Jesus about their day. He listens closely.

- At some point Jesus turns to you and gently invites you to share your good and bad experiences of the day.

- Remember, he is truly with you here and now.

To help you remember, ask yourself two questions:

1 WHAT WERE MY BEST,
MY HAPPIEST MOMENTS TODAY?

Tell Jesus about them. Tell him why you felt so happy
and thank him for those times.

> † *Lord Jesus, today was a great day,*
> *filled with friendship and joy.*
> *I thank you with all my heart,*
> *for giving me your Spirit of love.*

2 WHAT WERE MY WORST,
MY MOST DIFFICULT MOMENTS TODAY?

Tell Jesus about them, too. Try to figure out why you felt
so unhappy. If you happened to forget about God's law
of love, tell God you are sorry.

> † *Lord Jesus, you welcomed with kindness*
> *all the sinners who came to you;*
> *please forgive me my sins*
> *and help me be more faithful to your Spirit.*

Then ask Jesus to help you see how you could have more
of the best moments and less of the worst ones. This is
how Jesus will teach you, day by day, to follow the paths
of God. This is how he will share with you more and
more the joy of the Kingdom.

Get in the habit of ending your day by
praying to Mary, the mother of Jesus:

> † *Hail Mary, full of grace,*
> *the Lord is with you,*
> *blessed are you among women,*
> *and blessed is the fruit of your*
> *womb, Jesus.*
> *Holy Mary, Mother of God,*
> *pray for us sinners,*
> *now and at the hour of our death.*
> *Amen.*

OTHER PRAYERS FOR THE EVENING

Choose the ones that suit your mood and what happened today,
or find others at the end of this book (pages 120-128).

TO GIVE THANKS

† *O Lord, God almighty,*
  you do wonderful things for me:
  I can think and play, I can dream
  and make my dreams come true,
  I can make my own decisions,
  I can choose to love and make people happy.
  I thank you for the joy of being alive!

† *Lord Jesus, my friend, I had hard things to do today.*
  You stood by me all along and helped me do them.
  I love you and I thank you.

TO ASK FOR GOD'S HELP

We know God is not a magician who will change
things just to please us. But we also know that God
loves us even more than the most loving parent.
God will always help us find the light and courage
we need to go on with our life in hard times.

† *Dear God, I know you love me*
  and are always with me;
  I trust you.
  Please help me because...
  (Tell Jesus about your problem and ask for help.)

To understand better how God helps us, read the
story *How to survive hard times*, on page 62.

TO ASK FOR FORGIVENESS

† *Lord God, have mercy on me for I have sinned.*
  Because of your great love, forgive me and heal me.
  And my heart shall be new and filled with your joy!
  (Psalm 51)

IF YOU FEEL ANGRY

This prayer might help:

† *Lord Jesus, I am still angry because...*
  (tell Jesus what made you angry)
  Please help me to calm down so I can see how to make
  things right. Then help me to forgive and make peace
  so we can be friends again.

Then decide what you will do to make things right
and make peace in the next few days.

SHARING YOUR EVENING PRAYER WITH YOUR FAMILY

Why not ask your mom, your dad or your brothers or sisters to share your evening prayer sometimes? Jesus said:

When two or three gather in my name, I am there with them.
(MATTHEW 18:20)

Together we can help each other to pray better.

About once a week, Alec and Katie's whole family gathers around the kitchen table.

They light a candle to remind themselves that the Lord Jesus is truly with them.

They tell each other about the best and worst moments of the week. Imagine what each person might be saying...

Then together they give thanks to God and help one another see how to work for more of the "bests" and less of the "worsts"!

Families who do that once a week or so enjoy it very much. They learn a lot and grow closer to one another and to the Lord Jesus.

STAYING IN TOUCH WITH GOD THROUGH THE DAY

♥ A SECRET CONVERSATION THAT NEVER ENDS

Still no one there...

How often have you wanted to speak
to your parents or your best friend
but had to wait because they were not there?

God our Father, Jesus and the Holy Spirit
are always with us, so we can talk to them
at all times, day and night, and everywhere.
They always listen and always understand.

Look at the pictures on these two pages and
imagine what the people are saying to Jesus.

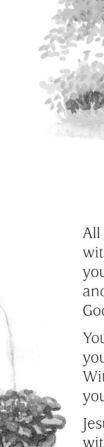

All day long, you can share everything
with Jesus: your joys and your hurts,
your fears and your hopes,
and your good laughs.
God surely has a good sense of humour!

You can even share your bad ideas,
your feelings of anger, jealousy or revenge.
With Jesus you never have to pretend;
you can always be just who you are.

Jesus will never be bored or angry
with what you tell him.

For the great Saint Teresa of Avila, sharing our thoughts with Jesus like that is the best way to grow closer to him.

But then, you might ask:
How does Jesus take part in the conversation?
First, just by being with you and listening to you. Knowing he shares your joys will make them even better. Knowing he understands your hurts or your fears will help you overcome them.

Through his Spirit he might bring peace to your heart and good ideas that will help you find the way out of your problems. See how he did this for Carol and her grandfather in the story on pages 72-75.

But God also speaks to us in many other ways:

♦ through the beauty of the world,

♦ through the people we meet,

♦ through those who help and comfort us,

♦ through the daily events in our lives.

All these experiences are opportunities to grow in faith and love, as you will discover in reading the stories starting on page 50.

Mr. Bala seems sad; I think I'll stop by on my way home from school.

If you keep your heart open, you will find out little by little that our loving God is with you every moment of your life. And that will bring you great joy! In the last part of this book, on page 125, there is a special prayer about that:
Lord, open my eyes...

♥ YOUR VERY OWN "TREASURE CHEST"!

Every one of us has a very special "treasure chest" that we bring everywhere with us...
That treasure chest is our memory and especially the memory of our heart.

Some things, like the things that happen to us, get into the treasure chest on their own.

Other things we can choose to put in, so we can find them when we need them. The more beautiful things you put into your heart, the more life-giving it will be.

PRECIOUS WORDS
FOR YOUR TREASURE CHEST

Jennifer is very sad. Her best friend, Lisa, moved away last week. But she keeps in her heart a few precious words that Lisa said to her when they said goodbye: *Jennifer, you are the best friend I ever had. I will always love you. I will write to you every month to keep in touch with you.* Whenever she feels sad, Jennifer remembers those words and they cheer her up.

Tony gets quite discouraged sometimes; he wonders if he will ever make it onto his town's hockey team. But then he remembers his grandpa's words: *Tony, I've been a coach for 30 years. I know you have what it takes to be a good player. Just keep working at it.*

We all keep in our heart some precious words from people who love and trust us. Remember words like these from someone in your own life.

Those words give you life, courage, hope, and joy; they are like a treasure you can go back to whenever you want.

WHAT ELSE CAN YOU PUT IN YOUR TREASURE CHEST?

You can put:
- ◆ memories of beautiful places or of happy moments like those Carol's grandpa shared with her (see pages 72-75),
- ◆ songs or poems you like,
- ◆ stories of Jesus that teach us how much God loves us,
- ◆ stories of wonderful people you meet in real life or hear about through books or TV.

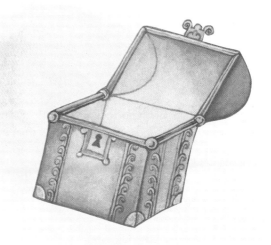

But you can also put in two other precious things:
- ◆ short lines from the Bible that bring you light and comfort,
- ◆ short prayers (some people call these "arrow-prayers" because they fly to God's heart like arrows!).

Here are some of these words from the Bible and short prayers. You might want to learn them by heart so they will come to your mind easily whenever you need them. This is what helped Kevin when he was wondering what to do about his new group of friends (see pages 51-53).

WORDS FROM THE BIBLE TO TREASURE

- *Do not be afraid. I am always with you.* (ISAIAH 41:10)
- *I love you with everlasting love; my love will never turn away from you.* (ISAIAH 54:8-10)
- *Follow the lead of the Spirit and you will not do wrong.* (GALATIANS 5:16)
- *Love one another as I have loved you.* (JOHN 15:12)
- *Happy are those who work for peace. They are truly children of God.* (MATTHEW 5:9)
- *God who raised up the Lord Jesus will raise us also by his power.* (1 CORINTHIANS 6:14)
- *Whatever you do, do it well in the name of the Lord Jesus.* (COLOSSIANS 3:17)

SHORT PRAYERS TO REMEMBER

- *Praise God, all people of the earth. Sing for God, who loves us so!*
- *Lord Jesus, you are my best Friend; I truly trust in your love.*
- *Lord God, I am calling for help. May your light shine upon me.*
- *Spirit of God, open my heart to your call; help me live in your love.*
- *Lord Jesus, you are my Shepherd, teach me to walk in your paths.*

ENJOYING NEW WAYS TO PRAY

Whenever we decide to set aside a little more time for God, it is good to try some new ways to pray. This will deepen our friendship with the Lord. The next few pages suggest some different ways to pray.

Remember, you are not alone in learning how to pray. God our Father gives us the Spirit of Jesus, the Spirit of love, to teach us how to pray. So each time you pray, start by asking the Holy Spirit to help you.

1 THE BREATH OF LIFE PRAYER

Maybe you have heard of the "breath of life" game. There is a way to turn this into a beautiful prayer. Enjoy it alone or with someone you love. Here is what you do:

- Sit down with your back straight. Close your eyes. Put your hands in your lap. Open your heart to the Spirit of Jesus. Breathe slowly and deeply three or four times. Sit still and stop breathing for a few seconds. You might feel a slight pounding in your chest. That is your heartbeat!

- Start breathing again very softly and deeply. Feel the air entering your body and giving it life again. Enjoy it. It is the breath of life God is giving to you, right here and now.

- Smile to relax your muscles. Then imagine you hear the voice of God telling you:
  You are precious in my eyes. I love you.
  I have called you by your name. You are mine.

- Repeat those words in your heart.
  Let them fill you with peace and joy as long as you feel like it.

- Open your eyes. Stand up slowly, raise your arms and give thanks to God our Creator for your breath of life. You might make up a prayer, sing a song or offer a dance to praise God.

> † **My heart sings to you, O Lord,**
>
>   **for the gift of my life, for the joy of your love.**
>
>   **My heart sings to you, O Lord!**

☑ THE JESUS PRAYER

Another way you can use your breath to pray is the "Jesus prayer." This is a very old way of praying that Russian pilgrims used a long time ago as they travelled to a shrine.

Start your prayer like the first one.

But this time don't stop breathing for a few seconds like in the first breath prayer.
Keep breathing gently.

– When you breathe in, say in your heart with love: **Jesus, my Lord,**

– when you breathe out, say whatever you want, for instance:

  - **have mercy on me,**
  - **please help me,**
  - **give me your peace.**

Do this for as long as you want.

This way of praying is easy to do: Valerie uses it often on her way to school. You can pray this way anytime, but if you are walking, keep your eyes open!

3 MEDITATION

What is meditation? Here are two examples:

- When you get a letter from someone you care about a lot, you don't read it just once. You keep it and read it many times, and you think about it, especially when you miss that person or when you feel sad.

- When you have seen on TV or read the story of a great person who makes you dream of doing great things yourself, you like to read over or remember that story. It helps you to grow and learn.

These are both a kind of meditation. Notice how the meditation unfolded. You made your body still, your mind and heart quiet. Then you could concentrate on thinking about someone who was very important for you. Meditating can become a wonderful way of growing in love with God, of getting to know Jesus better, of learning to live as friends of Jesus. There are many ways to meditate. Try them and enjoy them alone or with your friends.

MEDITATING ON A PRAYER

We often pray without really thinking about the words we are using. Meditating on that prayer can help us think about it better. For instance, this is how you might meditate on the first words of the *Our Father*.

Most often the word "father" reminds us of someone we love dearly and whom we call "daddy." But it might be that we have never known our daddy or that we have bad memories of him. Whatever the case, it helps us all to try to understand better what we mean when we call God "Our Father."

- As usual, calm your body, become quiet in your heart and ask the Spirit of Jesus to guide your prayer.

- Remember Jesus. Imagine him alone at dawn on the mountain where he often went to pray. Look at Jesus; stay close to him. Feel the peace and quiet happiness on his face when he speaks to God, saying with great love: *Abba, Father!*

- Imagine Jesus turning to you and saying gently: *My Father is also your Father, the Father of all. So when you want to pray to God, you will say "Our Father..."*

Our Father...

Repeat those words softly.
Let them fill you with wonder.

Yes, God, the Almighty,
the Creator of heaven and earth,
I can call that God "Father"...
It is God, our loving Creator
who gives me my breath of life
day after day.
God's love is forever,
it is stronger than death.

Yes, God's tender love for us
is even greater than the love
of the best of parents.

Our Father...

Repeat these words in your heart, and
let them fill you with peace and trust.

Who art in heaven...

This seems to mean, at first,
that God is very, very far away.
But that is not so. It is a way
to say that God belongs to
another world, a mysterious
world of light and joy. We will
enter this world when we die.

But Jesus also said: *Anyone*
who loves me, my Father will
love him. We will come to him
and make our dwelling place
with him. (JOHN 14:23) So
when we say *Our Father who*
art in heaven, we are speaking
to the God of love who dwells
in our heart.

Our Father who art in heaven...

Gently repeat those amazing words. Then speak to God our Father from
your heart, telling God of your love and trust, your wish to know God more
and more.

Hallowed be thy name...

When we say the name of someone who is very
dear to us, we say it with respect, love and joy.

Gently repeat God's name that way. Make up
your own names for God. Find them in your
heart!

Another day, you might meditate on the next
sentence of the *Our Father*, and so on. This will help
you understand this prayer better and better. Each
time you say it, it can bring you peace and joy.

MEDITATING ON A GOSPEL STORY

Choose a Gospel story that you like and know well. You may read it over or just remember it.

Tell the story to yourself as if you were going to make a movie about it.

♦ Imagine the story as if you were there: the place, the weather, the people.

♦ Look at what they are doing. Listen to what they are saying.

♦ Imagine what the people are feeling: fear? love? despair? hope? anger? happiness? Try to figure out why they have those feelings.

♦ When the story is finished, imagine Jesus standing close to you. What does he want to say to you, to teach you through this story? Listen in your heart, then say to Jesus whatever you want.

Let's take the story of Zacchaeus (LUKE 19:1-10) as an example. This is how you might start.

● Imagine you are there in the crowd on a busy street in Jericho. The sun is very hot.

● You feel a stirring in the crowd. Someone says: *It is Jesus coming down the road!* You can't see

Jesus yet, but you manage to climb on a large rock so you can see him.

● How is he dressed?

● How is he acting with the people?

● What is the expression on his face?

● How are people acting around him? Why are they there?

● Then you see a very short man trying very hard to see Jesus. It is Zacchaeus. Is he saying something? What? What is the expression on his face?

● Suddenly Zacchaeus sees a tree beside the road. He climbs high enough to see Jesus. What a smile the man has on his face!

● Jesus is there now. He stops right under the tree and looks up at Zacchaeus. What is the expression on Zacchaeus' face? What is he feeling?

Continue meditating on the rest of the story in your own way.

MEDITATING ON A QUOTE FROM THE BIBLE

Choose a short quote from the Bible that brings you joy, peace or courage. Here is an example: *I am the Light of the world. Whoever follows me will never walk in darkness but will enter the light of eternal life.* (JOHN 8:12)

♦ Prepare your body and mind as usual.

♦ Remember that Jesus is there with you.

♦ Repeat that quote in your heart as many times as you want.

♦ Then speak to Jesus. Ask him to help you understand it well:

    – *What is the darkness you talk about, Lord Jesus?*

    – *How can you be the Light of my heart?*

    – *How can I follow you more closely?*

After each question, sit quietly so you can hear in your heart what the Spirit of Jesus is saying to you.

When you feel sad or depressed, like Kathy in the story on pages 66-68, this way of praying can bring you great comfort.

When you meditate on a quote from the Bible, it becomes part of your "treasure chest." You might enjoy repeating it quietly in your heart during the next few days.

SILENT PRAYER

Sometimes you feel like praying, but you don't know what to say. So don't say anything. Just rest your heart in silence; God is there with you. Enjoy God's presence and peace. God is happy you are there! Sometimes it helps to make a gesture that shows your feelings.

4 PRAYING IN THE BEAUTY OF NATURE

Sometimes we don't notice all the beauty around us: the trees, the flowers, the animals, the sky, the clouds. Going for a walk, enjoying that beauty and praising God for it is a wonderful way to pray.

Whenever you get a chance to do this, you might like to end your day with one of the prayers on pages 120 and 121.

Here is a helpful hint. If you are in a bad mood, try going for a walk. The beauty of nature might help you relax, calm down and cheer up. Perhaps then you might even feel like praying to God, our loving Creator, who gives us this beautiful world to enjoy.

† *For the sun that gives life and fills our heart with joy, glory to you, Lord!*

5 PRAYING WITH THE BEAUTY OF ART

Artists can help us pray through their artwork. We must take the time to look at it with our heart so we can be touched by their message.

When we are tired and don't feel like saying much to the Lord, we might take a few minutes to pray quietly with a picture we love. You can try to do this with the picture on page 8.

6 PRAYING WITH MUSIC

You can do this in many ways:

- Sit quietly in your prayer corner and listen to your favourite religious music, resting your heart in God's loving presence.

- Sing a hymn as your morning or evening prayer.

- Make up a dance to go with a hymn or with some favourite music without words. Through your dance, show God the feelings in your heart.

CELEBRATING THE SACRAMENTS
IN OUR COMMUNITY

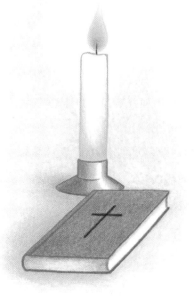

Sacraments are very special signs of God's love for us, very special ways to grow in love with God and with one another.

When we celebrate them together our faith grows stronger and we remember that as Christians we have promised to build a better world for everyone.

- Your parish might invite you to a community celebration of the sacrament of reconciliation, maybe during Advent or Lent. It would be great for you to take part, on your own or with your family or friends.

This sacrament is a time to remember God's calling and to reflect on our life. Praying together in this way helps us to follow Jesus more closely.

† *Bless the Lord with all your heart. He forgives all your faults, he crowns you with love and tenderness. Bless the Lord with all your heart.*
(Based on Psalm 103:1-4)

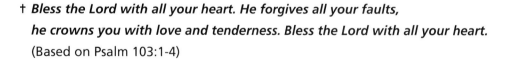

- Each week your community invites you to join in celebrating the Eucharist. Maybe sometimes you don't feel much like saying yes to that invitation. The following stories might help you understand why it's good to say yes.

A CHAT WITH MRS. BURNS

Mrs. Burns has a lot of trouble walking since the car accident in which her husband was killed a year ago. The Taylor family, who live nearby, visit her often and take her to Mass every Sunday.

Today, she thanked them even more warmly than usual:

Thank you for bringing me to Mass every Sunday. Along with your visits it is my favourite time of the week!

We enjoy bringing you, Mrs. Burns!

Suzy, who tends to be curious, asked:

Mrs. Burns, why do you like going to Mass so much? I often find it too long!

Remember, Lord, those who have died...

Another reason I like to go is that we all give thanks to God there. I have so many things to be thankful for: my 52 years of happiness with Paul, my lovely children and grandchildren, and wonderful friends like you!

~ Well, Honey, Mrs. Burns answered, *I'll tell you why. First of all, as you know, my children and grandchildren live far away. So when I find myself in the middle of all those lovely young families praying and singing together, it's as if all my family are there. That makes me happy.*

And there is a moment during the Eucharistic prayer when we mention our dear ones who have left us. We pray to be with them again in heaven forever.

At that time I feel so close to my dear Paul. It's as if he is reminding me that we will soon be together again. After all, I'm 76 already!

But you know, Mrs. Burns, you're like a third grandma to us!

You're so sweet, Suzy!

BRAVE STEPHANIE

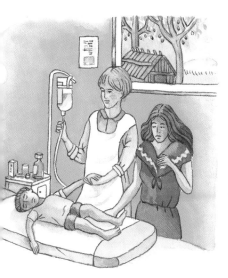

This is Stephanie's story. She is a doctor and has decided to spend one year helping poor people in Latin America. She has been in Mexico for two months where she works in a small clinic far out in the mountains.

She can't believe what is happening there! The mountain people have been chased away from their land by men with guns who are paid by rich farmers who say they own the land now. The people have formed small communities and are trying to work together so they can get their land back.

Catechists and social workers try to help the people in these small communities. But it is dangerous. Last week a catechist and a family with two children were killed by armed men as they walked to the village where the church and the clinic are.

But the next Sunday the church was full; again the people were as enthusiastic and the Mass as heart-warming as ever.

It had become a habit for Stephanie to gather after Mass with the catechists and social workers from the distant villages she had visited during the week.

Today, Padre Miguel joined them and said: *It would be better if you did not come to Mass for a week or two. It is too dangerous with those armed men out there.*

But the people said:

– Padre, don't even think of that! You know that coming here for the Eucharist gives us the courage to keep working for justice.

– We know we are risking our lives. But didn't Jesus do that too?

– Anyway, it is really when I share the Word and the Bread of Life with the whole community that I find the strength to continue my mission.

What about you? Did you know that after celebrating the Eucharist, you are sent off with a mission: to share the Good News of God's love and to build a better world around you?

Next time you don't feel like going to Mass, think about the people in these two stories and what makes the Eucharist so important.

PART TWO

LEARNING TO LIVE AS A FRIEND OF JESUS

Prayer makes our love for the Lord stronger and helps us answer his call. That is why the first part of your book was about prayer.

The second part will help you understand how to follow Jesus better. You will find that you can do this day by day, by growing as a person and by seeking the joy of God, the joy of the Kingdom.

You have felt that joy already. This is the joy we find when we trust in God, even when our life is hard, and when we try to build a better world together.

Two funny characters, Tic and Tac, will go along with you. They will often make you laugh, but they will also help you think. We hope you will enjoy their company!

Here they are presenting you with the three sections you will find in this second part of your book.

1. **What growing up is all about**
   (pages 35 to 49)

2. **Stories to enjoy and make you think**
   (pages 50 to 75)

3. **Helpful hints for a better life**
   (pages 76 to 83)

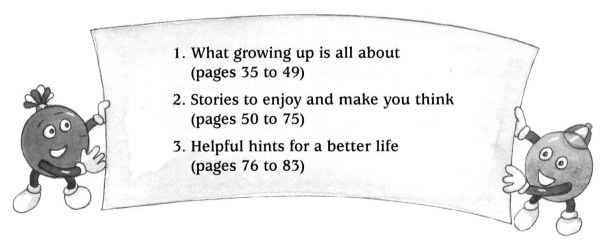

Look up the description of each section in the table of contents, on pages 2 and 3. This will help you choose the topic you want.

WHAT GROWING UP IS ALL ABOUT

1 LEARNING TO TAKE GOOD CARE OF OURSELVES

When we are born, we cannot take care of ourselves. We have to be fed, cleaned, clothed, and moved around.

As we grow up, we learn to take care of ourselves.

Now you are able to take care of yourself and be responsible for yourself in many ways. For example:

- When you need a snack, you can choose a healthy food.

- You get the sleep you need to stay in good shape.

- You ride your bike safely.

- You are smart enough to say "no" to things that can harm you.

No, thanks, that's bad stuff.

It's a good price...

I won't touch that. It can end up killing you.

❷ LEARNING TO LOVE OURSELVES

They're all alike!

It's terrible!

Imagine how boring life would be if we were all the same. Thank God, we're all different!

We each have special gifts: for studying, for music or drawing, for sports... It's important to work hard to develop these gifts.

We also have our own personality with good qualities and some faults.

Sometimes we envy other people's talents and good qualities and do not see our own. This makes us feel sad and discouraged.

That is why we often need someone to help see all our gifts and good qualities.

Bob is quite sad these days. He tries hard to learn but he is almost always last in school. He thinks that many of his classmates look down on him because of this. Even his dad seems disappointed. He would love Bob to be a good student and to become a doctor like he is.

Bob gets along very well with his older brother Jeff. One day, Bob shares his feelings:

I feel like I'm no good at anything and everyone knows it.

Jeff is stunned and shakes him up a little: *Come on, Bob, even if schoolwork is not your thing, you are able to follow the class. But you've got so many other gifts. You're the best at fixing things. Whenever there is something to repair or to build, everybody calls you. Even Dad had to ask you for help to fix his motorcycle the other day!*

Bob smiles a little: *Well, that was really easy to fix. Dad isn't the best mechanic!*

– But Bob, do you know how kind and generous you are? Look at the number of friends who call on you as soon as they have a problem. Remember the game we played last week in school: we had to choose the one person we would want to be with if we were shipwrecked on a desert island for two months and to explain our choice. You had the most votes in the whole school because you were the most resourceful and the best buddy! How can anyone like that feel sad?

Bob is starting to feel a bit silly listening to Jeff: *Thanks, buddy. You've opened my eyes. It's strange how sometimes we don't really know who we are! I guess I'll be able to find a job where I can use my hands and my heart, and not just my brains!*

– For sure, Bobby.

Nathalie is hopeless in sports and feels terrible about it. She is short and kind of clumsy. When there is a ballgame or a race she is always the last to be chosen.

One day, she tells her best friend, Laurie, how she feels.

I understand how you feel, says Laurie. But remember that whenever there is a party, you are the first to be invited because you are so full of life and fun. And when we put on a play, everybody wants to be on your team because you have so much imagination and act so well.

Thanks, Laurie. I feel better now. I guess we each have different talents. None of us can have them all!

Finally, Bob and Nathalie got their self-respect and self-confidence back. They learned to value themselves for who they are and to feel happy again. That's important, because if we do not love ourselves, we will find it very hard to love others.

You might take a moment here to think about two questions:

- Do I love myself as I am, with both my gifts and my limits? If not, who could help me to do that?

- Is there someone around me who might need my help to have more self-confidence?

If you want, you might end with this prayer:

† **God our loving Creator,**
   you are the source of all life.
   I thank you for the gift of myself,
   for my special talents and good qualities.
   Please help me use these gifts and good qualities
   not only for my own pleasure but also for others
   so we can all be happier.
   I ask this through Jesus, your Son. Amen.

3 IMPROVING OURSELVES

It is important to accept and value ourselves for who we are.
But it is also important to try to improve ourselves,
because we all have both good qualities and faults.

Clare and Sheila share a room. Clare is very kind, but she is so disorganized their room is almost always a mess! Sheila is very tidy and she gets mad at Clare for the mess.

Wow! What a mess!

Jason is very smart and always ready to help Clare and Sheila with their homework. But he is stubborn and sulks when he can't get his way.

Tony is very generous, but he gets angry over the silliest things. After that he is mad at himself.

Nothing is going right this morning!

Wouldn't life be better for the whole family if Clare, Sheila, Jason and Tony tried to work to overcome their faults?

HOW CAN I IMPROVE MYSELF?

The first thing to do is to try to know yourself better. This is one fun way of doing it.

- Interview the people who know you best and love you: members of your family, friends, teachers, catechists. Ask them to answer two questions:

  – What do you like most in my personality?

  – What would you suggest I improve about myself?

  Make sure you remember or write down their answers.

- Take some quiet time alone or with someone you are very close to and go over all that was said to you. Decide what you want to do to make your good qualities stronger and to improve yourself.

- Tell Jesus about the whole experience: how you feel about it and what you want to do now. Then ask Jesus for the courage to keep up your efforts to improve yourself.

4 UNDERSTANDING OUR FEELINGS BETTER

Feelings are a very important part of our life. In a single day we can go through a lot of feelings: hope, fear, jealousy, sadness, happiness, anger, shame, pride, guilt or excitement.

Look at the children on this page. Try to give a name to what each one is feeling. Then try to remember three or four different feelings you have had in the last few days.

Some feelings make us feel good; we can just enjoy them.

Other feelings upset us, like jealousy, fear, anger, sadness. What should we do about those feelings? We need to do two things:

– first, try to understand them better,

– then, decide how to find peace in our heart again.

UNDERSTANDING OUR UNPLEASANT FEELINGS

It is no use trying to fight a feeling and to push it back. It won't go away. What we need to do is learn to look at it and talk to it! Use your imagination and pretend your feeling is someone you can talk to.

Janice has two sisters: Maria is older, Rachel is younger. Then comes Martin, the baby. Today Janice feels upset and jealous. Imagine she is talking with the part of her that feels jealous. Listen to their conversation:

> Hello, Jealous, how are you?

> Bad! I'm sure Mom loves Maria more than she loves me.

– Why do you say that?

– Because Maria gets all the new things: coats, dresses, shoes, bikes, and when she's used them, Mom passes them down to me!

Janice understands where her feelings of jealousy come from. She does not have to feel guilty about them. Feelings just come to us; we are not responsible for them at the start. But now Janice will have to decide what to do about that feeling.

> What will Janice do now?

Janice can do two things:

- She can keep listening to Jealous and notice only all the little things that seem to show Jealous was right. For example, this morning Maria got to sit next to Mom in the front seat of the car. If Janice does this, she will feel worse and worse. She might even end up hating Maria and being mean to her.

- Or she can use her common sense and gently bring Jealous to see things differently:

You are wrong, Jealous. Even if I hate it, I understand why Mom has to pass down Maria's stuff to me sometimes. After all, there are three girls in our family. It would cost too much if we each had new clothes all the time.

During the next few days Janice could help Jealous notice all the little things in her life that show the special love and care Mom has for her.

On Monday she took Janice to the mall with her, while she asked Maria to watch Rachel and Martin at home, and Thursday she bought Janice her favourite treat.

Little by little Janice learns to deal with Jealous. Jealous has less and less to say, because Janice keeps showing her that she is wrong. Janice's life is getting much happier!

So when you have these kinds of feelings, do what Janice did. But if these feelings bother you too much, share them with someone who can help you.

It's also a good idea to share with Jesus all the feelings that trouble you. He will never be mad at you and will always understand you. Talking to him might help you feel peace in your heart again.

5 BECOMING A CARING PERSON

As we grow up, and especially when we share the Bread of Life, we begin to know what it means to follow Jesus by becoming a caring person like him. Being caring means **opening your eyes** to see what other people need. And it means **opening your heart** and doing what you can to help.

Justin and Hannah know that their mom, who is a night nurse, needs to sleep in the morning. They are very quiet when they're getting ready for school.

Mr. Peterson suffers from arthritis. He has trouble gardening. So Patrick, who lives nearby, often stops by to help him.

Annika makes sure that her friend Mary Rose is not left alone during recess. When the game is too hard for Mary Rose, Annika finds another game to play with her or sings a song with her.

It is not always easy to keep our eyes and heart open to other people's needs. But when we do try to become a caring person we find a very special kind of joy in our heart. This is the joy of God's Kingdom, a taste of God's own joy. It is a great gift!

To help you see what growing in love really means, read a story that Jesus told: The Good Samaritan. You can find it in your Bible (LUKE 10:29-37).

You might also meditate on these words of Jesus: *By this everyone will know that you are my disciples, if you have love for one another.* (JOHN 13:35)

Don't be a couch potato! There is so much more to life than TV and video games. There are so many wonderful things to discover and to enjoy in this world!

Keep your curiosity alive. Learn, discover,
experience new things and develop new skills.
Your life will bloom!

This is how we reacted when we were babies and could not do or have what we wanted.

But as we grow up we discover we have the power to control ourselves. Even if we are hungry we will not scream or cry. We will wait for dinner to be ready.

Sometimes two or three of us want to have or do the same thing at the same time.

But later on, we learn to talk about it and to share.

It is very important to strengthen our power of self-control – if we don't do this, we will end up fighting all the time. If we can't control our desires or accept disappointments, we could get into trouble – even stealing or hurting others to get what we want.

When we have some self-control, we can take the time to think about what we feel like doing and decide if it is right or wrong. This power to make good choices is a great gift.

As she walked out of a shopping mall, Jennifer saw something falling out of a woman's purse.

She picked it up – it was a $20 bill! Part of her wanted to put it in her pocket.

But she was able to control her desire and decided it was wrong. She ran after the woman to give the money back to her. The woman was so happy she gave Jennifer $2 to thank her!

Well done!

You can be proud of yourself when you gain more self-control and freely make good choices even when it is hard. This is a sign that you are growing up.

There is another very special and wonderful gift you may have discovered or will soon discover in your own body: the gift of your sexuality.

This gift can bring you great happiness if you use it as God intends: with respect, care and at the right time.

But it can also bring you great unhappiness and serious problems if you use it too soon. Ask your parents or other adults you respect and trust to tell you more about this wonderful power God has given us; ask them also how and when you should use it.

8 BECOMING RESPONSIBLE AND TRUSTWORTHY

Michael's family moved to Texas a few months ago. He is eleven years old now and he has much more freedom than when he was nine. He can ride his bike alone to the house of his best friend, Adam, and he can stay overnight. His parents know he is a very safe rider and does his homework with Adam. They trust him.

But one day, during the Christmas holidays, Michael discovered he had more to learn about being trustworthy.

On Saturday morning the phone rang. It was Marie, one of his parents' friends in a nearby town. Her husband had just had a serious accident. She asked Michael's mom and dad to come right away.

Dad asked Michael if he could take care of Tina, his little sister, for the day. Michael said yes.

Mom told him that Tina was quite tired after all the excitement of Christmas and that she would need a long nap in the afternoon. She said that Michael shouldn't leave the house in case Tina woke up and needed something. *Okay*, said Michael, *I won't leave the house.*

The morning went by fast. Michael and Tina had fun playing with their new toys and games. Michael made them some lunch, then Tina asked to take her nap right there on the living room couch near the Christmas tree. Michael said okay and started reading a new book so he wouldn't make any noise.

About half an hour later Adam came to Michael's door, all excited:

A.: *Mike, look at my new bike. You should come and try it.*

M.: *I can't leave the house. Tina is taking her nap. If she wakes up and I'm not there, she might be afraid. We can do it later when she's awake and I can leave her with the neighbours for a few minutes.*

A.: *But I have to go to my grandmother's later. Look, she's sound asleep. It'll only take two or three minutes. I'll take your bike and you try mine. We'll just race down the street and be back in no time.*

Mike looked at Tina. She did seem sound asleep.

M.: *Okay, but just for three minutes.*

A.: *Come on!*

M.: *Great!*

The three minutes turned out to be almost six minutes.

When Michael got back to his front door he could smell smoke. He rushed to the living room. The large paper rocks supporting the Christmas crib were on fire! Tina was hiding behind the couch, crying.

Mike remembered something he had heard when the firefighters had come to visit his school. He grabbed Tina's blanket and quickly threw it over the fire to put it out.

It turned out that Tina woke up when Michael shut the front door as he went out. She got up and felt like lighting the big candle near the Christmas crib. She climbed on a chair to reach the matches on top of the bookshelf and tried to light the candle, but the match fell on the paper rocks and set them on fire.

Then he ran to Tina and hugged her, saying:

It's okay, Tina, don't be afraid, it's okay.

Michael was very upset. He realized how irresponsible he had been. If Tina had been quicker to get the matches or if he had stayed away one minute more, the fire might have spread. Tina could have been badly hurt.

The best way to become trustworthy in important things is to be responsible in small things, like taking care of a pet, cleaning up if you make a mess, keeping your word or coming home on time.

Being responsible sometimes means giving up something you want. But it's worth it! This is how we decide to be more like Jesus.

STORIES TO ENJOY AND MAKE YOU THINK

In this section you will find real-life stories about young people who are dealing with different situations. You might be going through some of the same things. Their stories can help you see better how to grow as a person and as a disciple of Jesus.

- How to choose our friends

- What to do when we have a problem

- How to handle our anger

- How to make our world a better place for all

- How to find peaceful solutions to conflicts

- How to cope with the death of someone we love

- What to do about bullies

I love these stories, especially the one about Blue Pond.

I like the one about the grandpa best.

- How to survive hard times

Share these stories with your family or friends. Questions at the end of each story will help you talk about them together.

1 HOW TO CHOOSE OUR FRIENDS

Ruth, Neil and Kevin moved to a new town this summer, and can't wait to make new friends.

When Ruth started dance class, she met two nice girls who love dancing as much as she does. They get along well. Now they go to the park together almost every day to chat and swim with other friends. Once a week they go teach dance to mentally handicapped children.

Neil has met a bunch of guys who love sports; they play soccer and basketball. Because they are generous and like to be busy, they get involved in what's going on in the neighbourhood. They've become good friends.

Kevin hasn't found his place yet. He wanders around the neighbourhood feeling lonely. One day he sees a group of boys having great fun with the latest models of remote control cars. He gets closer to look and Eric, who seems to be the oldest and the leader, invites him to join them. *It would be fun to be friends with them*, Kevin thinks to himself. *They've got a lot of stuff.*

The next day he goes back and they invite him to play again. Then Eric asks Kevin to join them the next Saturday at the shopping mall to play at the video arcade.

They all meet there. Eric makes them split into pairs. While Kevin and Dan play at the arcade, the others will look around at the stores. The boys seem to have a lot of money to spend; they come back with all kinds of cool stuff and offer Kevin a new gadget. Then they buy everyone a big snack.

During the week, Kevin spends most of his time with Eric, Dan and the others. They have a good time. Someone always brings new games or stuff to play with. But Kevin is not really at ease in the group: *Where do they get all their money?* he wonders.

One day, Kevin talks to Jesus about it. He remembers a line from the Bible he had meditated on a few weeks before: *"Let the Spirit lead you and you will do no wrong"* (GALATIANS 5:16). He opens his heart and asks the Spirit to guide him.

A few days later, Kevin is at the mall with his dad. Suddenly he sees Dan in the next aisle. He is putting into his pocket a new $15 electronic game that Kevin had just looked at. Dan picks up another game and goes to the counter to pay for it. Kevin is stunned.

Later on, while waiting for his dad in the parking lot, Kevin sees a boy playing with the same electronic game Dan had stolen. As he passes by, Kevin says:

– Wow! That's a fun game.

– Yeah, says the boy, *and I got it at a discount!*

– How?

– Well, I met a guy named Dan who told me his uncle had bought it for him but he didn't like it; so he sold it to me for $10 instead of $15. Isn't that great?

– I guess so.

Kevin was very upset. So that's how the boys got all those games and that money: they were shoplifting. He decided right away to stop hanging around with them. He would tell the whole story to his family to talk about what to do; he would also look for other boys to hang out with.

QUESTIONS TO THINK ABOUT AND DISCUSS

1. What did Ruth and Neil do to find new friends?

   • Why did it work out so well?

   • Has anything like this happened to you? If so, share the story.

2. Why did Kevin choose to join Eric's group?

   • Was this a good reason? Why?

   • Would you like other kids to become your friend only because you have fun games or a swimming pool in your yard?

   • For what reasons would you like people to choose you as a friend?

3. Have you ever had to leave a group because you didn't agree with what the kids were doing? Was it hard to leave? How did it turn out?

4. What might have happened to Kevin if he had not been brave enough to leave the group?

   • Do you know kids who have been through something like this? Share their stories.

   • What did Kevin learn by going through this? How did he grow up?

5. Share what you have learned from this story by answering these questions:

   • How should we choose our friends?

   • Which mistakes should we avoid?

2 HOW TO HANDLE OUR ANGER

Mark is John's best friend. One day, on the way home from school, Mark made fun of John, imitating the way he had missed his jump at gym that day. Some other kids who were watching laughed loudly. John, who wishes he were better at sports, got so angry he dropped his backpack and tried to hit Mark. But Mark ran away too fast.

Back home, John was so mad he told his mom: *That's it! I won't be friends with Mark anymore. I'm going to get back at him. I'm going to tear up his favourite comic book he lent me last week. I'll bring the pieces to him at school tomorrow!*

John's mom got him a cold drink and listened to the story. Then she said: *You know how Mark is. He's really a good buddy, but he can't resist making fun of things or people for a laugh. You laugh with him sometimes, don't you?*

– *Yeah, but he knows how mad I get when I miss my jumps. When it's my turn to be laughed at, it hurts!*

– *It sure does. But tearing up his book won't make him change.*

– *I guess you're right, but I want him to know how mad and hurt I was.*

– *Let him know. But wait a bit till you have calmed down. Go play with the dog for a while.*

So John took the dog for a walk. He remembered all the good times he and Mark had had together, and the times Mark had helped him. John realized that Mark really was a good friend.

So after dinner, when he felt better, he called Mark and told him about feeling angry and hurt. Mark said he was sorry and that he didn't mean to hurt John; he was just having fun.

The next morning Mark brought John a video he had wanted to borrow; it was his way to make up and be friends again. As they walked to school they chatted and Mark said:

You know, John, maybe I should be more careful about laughing at things and people. I could end up losing my best friends.

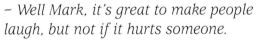

– Well Mark, it's great to make people laugh, but not if it hurts someone.

– You're right. I'll try to remember that. You can help me!

– Okay.

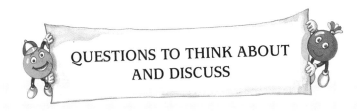

1. Mark's teasing did not seem so mean at first. But John felt upset and hurt. Why?

   - Did someone ever make fun of your weak points? How did you feel? Why? Share your experiences.

   - Is anyone in your family, school or neighbourhood made fun of for their weak points?

   - What might happen to that person if this goes on? Can you do something about it?

2. Often, when we get mad, the first thing we want is to get revenge. Is this the best way to react? Share your experiences.

   - What might have happened if John had rushed to his room to tear up Mark's comic book right away?

   - When John went to the kitchen where his mom was, what helped him calm down?

   - How do you calm down if you're mad?

3. It's okay to be angry. We all have good reasons sometimes to get angry. But then we need to forgive and make peace.

   - What is forgiving about? Talk about these two ideas:

     – Forgiving is pretending that nothing happened and that things are okay, even if they are not.

     – Forgiving is, after we have calmed down, expressing our anger without violence, talking things over and then making peace.

   - Which idea sounds better to you? Why?

   - Imagine that John had pretended that everything was okay. What would have happened to his friendship with Mark?

4. We all have problems with our friends sometimes. A good friendship is worth a lot – if something goes wrong, we need to work hard to fix it instead of throwing it away.

   - Did you ever end a friendship because you were not able to forgive? How do you feel about it now?

   - What could you have done then to stay friends?

   - Jesus had problems with his friend Peter. (MARK 14:29-31; JOHN 21:15-17) Share what you remember about that story. How did Jesus act towards Peter?

5. If you feel like it, end your discussion with the prayer "For my friends" (page 125).

***Don't let the sun
set on your anger.***
(EPHESIANS 4:26)

3 HOW TO FIND PEACEFUL SOLUTIONS TO CONFLICTS

Jan's family lives in a new and growing suburb near a beautiful forest. An amazing variety of birds and little animals live in the area.

One day a large group of neighbourhood children went to the woods to clean up a little pond called Blue Pond. When they got there they saw another group of kids who were throwing stones at the birds, catching frogs and hurting them, and throwing dead wood into the pond. The group that had come to clean up got very angry and tried to stop the others. It all ended in a big fight.

The same thing happened again during the week. So Jan, Maya, Alan and all their friends decided to hold a meeting the following Sunday after Mass to talk about what to do.

They each told Jesus about their anger and asked him to help them find a peaceful solution to the problem.

During the meeting, Maya said, *They're just a bunch of troublemakers! We should report them to the police.*

Jan thinks they should first try to understand why these kids were acting as they did: *Maybe they are just bored because the playgrounds aren't built yet.*

Alan agrees with Jan. He was struck by a line from this Sunday's Gospel: "Don't judge others and you will not be judged" (LUKE 6:37). He wonders if anyone ever taught these kids to respect the environment and enjoy the animals.

After talking for a long time, the group came up with some great ideas for how to fix the problem. Alberto's family had a friend named Mrs. Cairns who had lived in the area for 30 years. She was an artist and loved nature. Over the years she had painted all the birds and little animals that lived in those woods; she had an amazing collection of paintings. *So why not put up an exhibit*, they all cried out together!

With the help of their teachers and parents, the children organized an art exhibit in the gym of their new school to display Mrs. Cairns' beautiful paintings. Under each painting, a card gave the name of each bird and animal and said a few things about it.

The children asked the local newspaper and TV station to announce the exhibit. It was to open the following Sunday afternoon. Those interested in helping to take care of Blue Pond and the woods would hold a meeting to share ideas after the exhibit.

The exhibit was a big success! Many families came, including those of the kids who had caused trouble at the pond. Everyone was amazed at the beauty of the birds and animals. Many stayed for the meeting.

Jan, Alan and their friends said "Hi" to the kids they had fought with and asked them to join the new club. Many said they would because they had never really paid attention to birds and animals before. They would know better now.

A city councillor suggested that adults and children form a club to clean up and take care of the woods and the pond. They would build wooden benches where people could sit quietly to watch the birds and all the little animals coming to drink at the pond.

Mrs. Cairns was delighted that her paintings had helped people become aware of the beauty around them. She offered to teach the children in the club about other birds and animals that she had painted during her many trips around the world. They became great friends.

QUESTIONS TO THINK ABOUT AND DISCUSS

1. Did Jan and her friends have good reasons to get mad when they got to Blue Pond that day?

   - What was their first reaction?

   - What came out of it?

2. When the group talked about it, they had two choices:

   – get revenge on the other kids, or report them;

   – try to understand why the other kids acted the way they did and find a creative way to change their behaviour.

   - What would probably have happened if they had chosen the first way?

   - Why was it good that they chose the second way?

     – for the environment?

     – for Jan and her friends?

     – for the kids who caused the trouble?

     – for the community as a whole?

3. Did you ever see a group of kids doing something wrong, like beating someone up, stealing, using drugs, or harming the environment?

   - How did you react?

   - If you did nothing, why? If you did try something, what happened?

4. Share your feelings about this story by talking about these ideas:

   - Getting people of different generations to work together to improve life in a neighbourhood is a great way to build community spirit. This makes a better world for all, which is exactly what following Jesus is about!

   - Is there a good opportunity to act creatively as a group in your own neighbourhood?

4 WHAT TO DO ABOUT BULLIES

In Matthew's new class there is a bully named Paul. He is tall and strong and always wears expensive clothes. From the first day, Paul spotted Ryan, who is shy and not too tall, wears ordinary clothes, and is not very good at sports. Paul is always making fun of Ryan, playing tricks on him or beating him up. Because Ryan is smart and gets good marks, Paul says he cheats.

Paul tries to get the whole class to join him in the bullying. Some do because they are scared of Paul and jealous of Ryan. When Matthew tries to defend Ryan he gets bullied, too.

Matthew talks to Jesus about this problem during his evening prayer and asks him what to do. He remembers what Jesus said to his friends: *Whatever you do to the least of my brothers and sisters, you do unto me* (adapted from MATTHEW 25:40).

So one day, Matthew and his best friend, Dan, decide to talk about the problem with all the other boys who have not yet joined in the bullying. They agree it's not fair to let Ryan be bullied. They talk about how they will stand up to Paul together, and they invite Ryan to be part of their group.

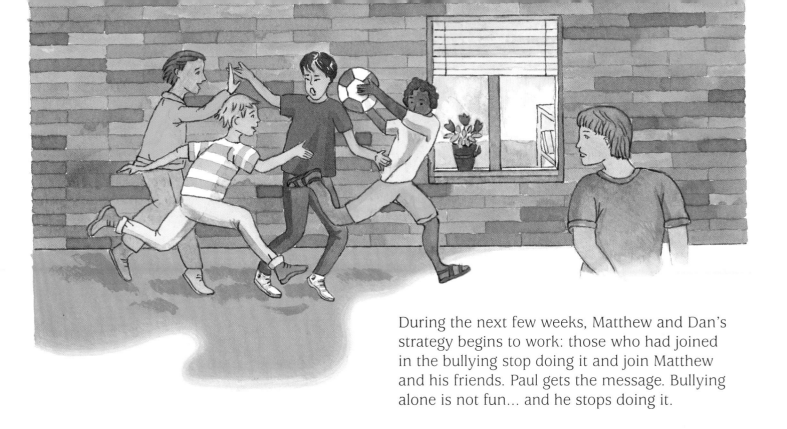

During the next few weeks, Matthew and Dan's strategy begins to work: those who had joined in the bullying stop doing it and join Matthew and his friends. Paul gets the message. Bullying alone is not fun... and he stops doing it.

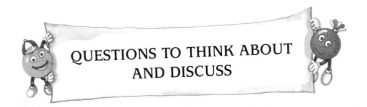

QUESTIONS TO THINK ABOUT AND DISCUSS

1. Have you ever been bullied?
   - How did you feel about it?
   - What did you do? How did it all end?

2. Has a group of bullies ever stolen your things or your money and said they would get you if you told on them? How did you get them to stop?

3. Have you ever acted as a bully yourself?
   - What made you do it?
   - How did it all end?

   - If you are ever tempted to do it again, just ask yourself two questions:
     – How would I feel if I was in the place of the kid I want to bully?
     – Does bullying fit into the better world that Jesus wants us to build with him?

4. End your reflection by talking about these questions:
   - Is anyone in your school or neighbourhood being bullied? How could you help?
   - When do kids need to ask adults (parents, teachers, social workers or police) to help stop bullying or violence?

Do to others what you would have them do to you. (LUKE 6:31)

For the last few months, Karina, Nick and Gerry's parents had been arguing more and more often. Everybody was very tense at home.

Four weeks ago, their parents told them they were going to get a divorce because they could no longer get along and it would be better for everybody. Soon after Daddy left home and went to live at the other end of town.

It was quieter at home; Mom seemed calmer but the children were very upset. Everything seemed to be going wrong since the separation. They all had trouble in school.

They missed their dad a lot. They spent every other weekend with him but they were all confused, having two homes and never knowing where they had left their stuff.

Dad wasn't around anymore to fix things in the house or to repair Gerry's bike or Nick's rollerblades.

The children felt kind of angry all the time but they were ashamed to talk to anyone about it. Nick was sick a lot and Gerry had awful nightmares. Karina often woke up crying.

Finally, one day, Nick decided he would talk to Ted, his best friend. Ted's parents had gotten divorced two years ago, so Nick thought he might understand: *I have a terrible secret to share with you, Ted. But promise me you won't tell anyone.*

After hearing the news, Ted said he was sorry this had happened. Then he said: *It helped our family a lot to talk with the school counsellor, Mrs. Lynch. If you want, I will take you to meet her. Let's go and see if she is in her office.*

The three children prayed together at night, asking Jesus to bring their daddy home and to help them get their lives back together again.

So they went to see her and she told Nick to come and talk to her the next day.

Nick told Mrs. Lynch all about the divorce and how terrible they all felt:

I think it might be my fault because I made my dad mad sometimes and was no good at math.

But Mrs. Lynch said:

Nick, it is never the children's fault when parents divorce. Adults have their own problems. Sometimes when they are not able to solve them and life becomes too hard for everyone in the family, it's better for them to separate.

Mrs. Lynch told Nick that he could come back the next day with Karina and Gerry if they wanted to chat. So they did. They all shared their feelings of anger, guilt and sadness. Mrs. Lynch was very kind and understanding. Then she added:

If it's okay with you, I will call your mom and dad and invite them to come to see me too. Maybe I could help everybody cope with the situation and support one another better through these hard times.

The next year was still quite hard for the children, but anytime they wanted they could call Mrs. Lynch and talk with her. This helped them and it helped their mom and dad, too.

They all adjusted to the new situation as best they could. Although the pain would always remain, they each found a way to be happy again and to enjoy one another. Their mom and dad were both very loving parents and the children learned to understand them better and respect their feelings as grown-ups.

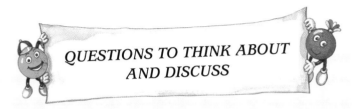

QUESTIONS TO THINK ABOUT AND DISCUSS

Sometimes we go through hard times like Karina and her brothers did. It might be a broken friendship, a failure in school or in sports, someone spreading rumours about us, or health problems. We may feel too upset, sad, guilty or ashamed to talk about it to anyone.

1. If you have ever gone through hard times, try to answer these questions:

   • What was the hardest thing about this time?

   • What helped you get through it?

   • Why are we sometimes afraid to tell someone how we are feeling?

2. Why is it so important that we share our feelings with someone we trust?

   What might have happened to Karina and her brothers if Nick had not talked to his friend Ted?

3. End your reflection by talking about these ideas:

   • The three children prayed for their father to come back and for life to go back to normal. But this did not happen.

     – Did Jesus answer their prayers? How?

     – Whom did he use to help them?

   • Do you know someone who is going through a hard time and needs special care? If you do, pray for a moment, asking the Spirit of Jesus to help you see what you could do about it.

6 WHAT TO DO WHEN WE HAVE A PROBLEM

Kathy never knew her father. She had always lived with her mom, who worked very hard to give her a good life. They lived in a nice apartment with a large balcony and Kathy was very happy.

One day, her mom told her they would be moving in with James, a very good friend of hers who was raising his two children, Ben and Rebecca, on his own. James and her mom loved each other and wanted to try to build a new family together.

For three months now, Kathy and her mom had lived with James, Ben and Rebecca. James was very nice to Kathy and she got along okay with the kids. She had her own room, but it was a completely different life and Kathy found it hard to get used to it.

She became quite sad, had a hard time doing her schoolwork, and didn't join the games at recess. She often cried when she was alone with her best friend, Angela, who got very worried because Kathy wouldn't say what was wrong.

Finally, one day Kathy told her: *You know, Angie, I don't think my mom loves me as much now. I think she cares for Ben and Rebecca more than me.*

– What makes you say that, Kathy?

– Well, for one thing, when she comes to our rooms in the evening to say good night, she stays longer with them than with me. And they are allowed to read or watch TV later than me. They get bigger pieces of dessert, and she buys them better stuff for their lunches. It's not fair!

– *Kathy, I'm sure she does not love them more than you, but I think you should talk to her and tell her how you feel. Let her explain.*

– *I'm afraid she'll be mad at me; she'll think I'm jealous.*

– *I bet she'll understand. You know how much she wants you to be happy.*

Kathy did what Angie said. That evening, when her mom came to say good night, Kathy started crying. Her mom held her and asked what was wrong. Kathy shared all her feelings and her mom explained to her many things:

Honey, you know you are my very own little girl and I love you more than anybody else! Of course, I love Ben and Rebecca too. Sometimes I stay a few minutes longer with them, but it's just so I can get to know them better. I want to be a good stepmother for them. I let them stay up a little later at night because they were used to that. I can't ask them to change all their habits at once, can I?

As for the lunch boxes, I try to buy their favourite cookies. But have you noticed that whenever I have time, I bake just for you, your own favourite cookies?

Mom ended the conversation by teasing her little girl with a smile:

When it comes to bigger pieces of dessert, I think that comes from the imagination of a greedy little dessert lover whom I know so well and love so much! Kathy laughed and hugged her mom. Now she felt better. She told her mom there were a lot of things she liked about being a larger family after all.

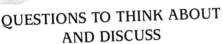

QUESTIONS TO THINK ABOUT AND DISCUSS

1. How did Kathy feel when her mom told her they would be moving in with James?

   Why is it scary when big changes happen in our life? Share a time when this happened to you.

2. What might have happened to Kathy if she had not told her friend how she was feeling and finally talked to her mom?

   Have you or some of your friends gone through something like this?

3. Why is it a bad idea to keep our feelings inside when we are sad or worried?

4. Why did Kathy feel so good after talking with her mom?

5. Share what you have learned from this story by discussing these questions:

   • Kathy was used to having her mom all to herself. She found it hard to "share" her with James, Ben and Rebecca. How did that experience help her grow up and make her life better?

   • When we are sad or worried but don't tell anyone, we feel very alone. It is like being in a cage; we can't fully enjoy life. Do any of your friends seem to need your help to confide in someone? What could you do about it?

Carry each other's burdens, says the Bible. (GALATIANS 6:2)

Mercedes and Pedro Mendez live in a large housing project in the inner city. Life is quite tough there. There is violence and drugs. The buildings are not well taken care of, the elevators are often out of order, people are very careless and the stairways are dirty. Nobody ever bothers to recycle anything, and the garbage cans are always overflowing. The Mendez family would like to move to a better place but they don't have enough money yet.

One Saturday morning Pedro hears a loud noise in the stairway. Someone is crying for help! He and his dad rush out and see Mrs. Murphy, an older lady who lives on the 4th floor, lying at the bottom of the stairs. She had slipped on some garbage and tumbled down the stairs. It looks like she has broken her leg. She is in terrible pain.

Dad tells Pedro to call 911 while he stays with Mrs. Murphy. While she is in the hospital, the Mendez family takes care of her cat, waters her plants, and visits her often. They all become good friends.

A lot of things are happening during that time. Mercedes, Pedro and three of their friends decide to do something about the mess on the stairs. After talking to their parents, they write a letter to all the tenants of stairway "B." They tell people what happened to Mrs. Murphy and invite them to join in a big clean-up day for their stairs. They slip the letter under every door.

On the clean-up day, the weather is sunny and almost every family helps.

Mr. Thomas, who works in a hardware store, has brought some paint and brushes. There is a lot of sweeping, dusting, scrubbing, fixing and washing. Everyone is in a good mood! Mrs. Glenn, who works in a flower shop, even brought a beautiful plant to put at the bottom of the stairs next to a large garbage can. A bright, cheerful poster reminds everyone to keep the stairway clean and to recycle.

At the end of the day, everyone is tired but happy with the job they did. They all give a cheer: Hip, Hip, Hurray!

Mrs. Mendez says they should have a party to celebrate. She suggests they all meet in a nearby park for a pot-luck barbecue the next day at noon. Everyone says it's a great idea. This is the day Mrs. Murphy will be coming home from the hospital. Mrs. Mendez will go and get her. When Mrs. Murphy gets home, she is so surprised! She can't believe her eyes when she sees the stairs.

The barbecue is great. People of all ages enjoy getting to know each other better. They share their concerns and ideas about life in the housing project. They all promise to keep the stairways clean.

Some adults who have noticed that the grounds need work, too, have decided to clean them up. They have also decided to form a committee to meet with the police about how they can help get drugs out of the housing project.

Pedro, Mercedes and their friends visit Mrs. Murphy every day and help her with many little things. One day, she invites them over for a snack, saying she has a surprise for them:

Since my husband died two years ago, she said, there is a large room in the back of the apartment that I don't use. It was his workshop. All his things are still there. There is a door leading to the hallway. If you want, you could use that room for activities. I even have a friend who could teach you to do some crafts if you like.

The children were thrilled! They hugged Mrs. Murphy and thanked her. They decided that in return they would help Mrs. Murphy with her cleaning, her grocery bags and her laundry every week.

It is amazing how life on stairway "B" has changed since Mrs. Murphy's accident!

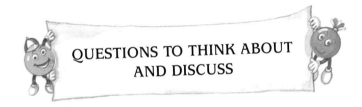

QUESTIONS TO THINK ABOUT AND DISCUSS

Sometimes good things can come out of an accident, but it's too bad we wait for them to happen before we take action to make things better!

1. Stairway "B" had been in bad shape for a long time and most of the tenants were unhappy about it. Why didn't anyone do anything about it before the accident?

   Have you known a time when nobody would get involved to solve a problem?

2. Name all the good things that came out of the children's ideas for making things better:

   – for Mrs. Murphy

   – for the other tenants

   – for the children themselves.

3. Has anything like this ever happened to you or someone you know? Share the stories.

4. Share what you have learned from the story by discussing these questions:

   • If we keep our eyes open, if we use our imagination and take action, we can make a big difference. That is what Jesus dreams of when he invites us to work together for a better world for all. It can be lots of fun!

   • Do you know of something in your neighbourhood that needs fixing? What could you and your family and friends do about it together?

8 HOW TO COPE WITH THE DEATH OF SOMEONE WE LOVE

Carol's family is going through a hard time. Her grandma died two weeks ago of a heart attack. She lived with Carol's grandpa a few blocks away. Carol used to stop by there almost every day on her way home from school.

Carol is so sad, she has only stopped by at Grandpa's house once since Grandma died and she did nothing but cry and cry. At home she's very upset; she doesn't want anybody to talk about Grandma. She doesn't want to join in the family prayer anymore. At school she hides during recess instead of playing.

One evening, when her mom comes to kiss her good night, she takes Carol in her arms and says:

Carol, I want to talk to you. You can't go on like this.

Carol bursts into tears and they talk for a long time. Carol says she is angry with God because he took her grandma away.

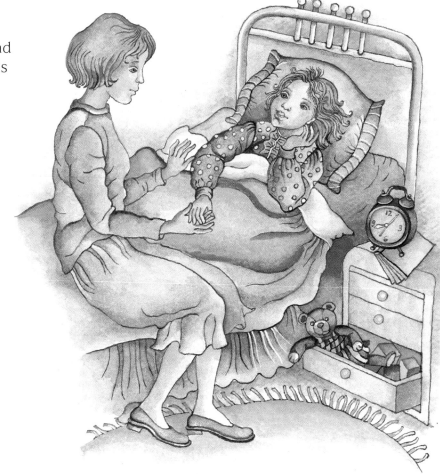

God didn't do that, Mom explains. *Grandma was old and had a sick heart. That's why she died. But it's okay to tell God you are angry; God will understand.*

Then they talk about Grandpa:

Carol, you know how much Grandpa needs all our love to help him cope with his terrible sadness. He misses your visits so much.

I know you find it hard to talk about Grandma and to go to her house, but can you try to do it for Grandpa? Maybe you could help one another.

They pray together, asking Jesus to give Carol the love and courage she needs to overcome her own pain and to try to comfort her grandpa.

The next day after school, Carol prays to Jesus all the way to her grandpa's house. When Grandpa sees her, he hurries to meet her, takes her in his arms and they cry together for a while.

Then Grandpa says: *Come on, Carol, I need help to take care of Grandma's favourite flowers. I want to keep them beautiful!* So they work in the flower bed and talk about Grandma.

When they are finished and are having a cold drink, Carol says: *I wonder what it's like in heaven. Why don't we know more about it? Did you ever talk with Grandma about that?*

– *We did. We talked about it twice before she died. Do you know what she said?*

– *Please tell me!*

– The first time was after Thanksgiving dinner. We had had a wonderful day with you and your uncles, aunts and cousins. On the way home she said: "You know, Peter, sometimes I think heaven must be something like that: a wonderful family feast with all the people you love, with God and the saints, but it would last forever."

– Wow! That's a nice thought. What did she say the second time?

– The second time was when your mom came to tell us four months ago that she was pregnant. It reminded Grandma of the time, 35 years ago, when she was expecting your mom. She shared with me something she had never talked about before.

– What was it?

– She said: One day I was sitting in the rocking chair and I was feeling my little baby moving gently in my womb. Suddenly it occurred to me that this little baby had no idea what a wonderful world and life was waiting for her after her birth. It would be a complete surprise! And I thought to myself: "Maybe dying is like being born: we have no idea where we are going but we're in for a big surprise!"

– Maybe a wonderful surprise?

– Well, we know that Jesus promised us eternal joy in God's new world.

– I love these stories about Grandma. It's as if she is here with us, Grandpa!

– In a way she is, because she is with God and I feel she is very close, so I speak to her often.

From that day on, Carol kept in her treasure chest, in the memory of her heart, those two stories about her grandma. Whenever she heard that someone had died, she would meditate for a moment on her grandma's words: *We are in for a big surprise!* And then she felt better.

She has even done a drawing of her grandma as a mother-to-be in her rocking chair. She put the drawing in her prayer corner with these words of Jesus: "I will prepare a place for you."

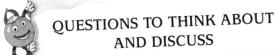

QUESTIONS TO THINK ABOUT AND DISCUSS

1. Why do you think Carol did not want to talk about her grandma or visit her grandpa?

2. When someone we love dies, we feel very sad. Has someone you loved very much died?
   - How did you feel?
   - What helped you to feel better?

3. When we are in great pain, we sometimes are ashamed to cry. But crying is quite natural. Sometimes crying together can help us heal. Jesus cried when his friend Lazarus died.

   Other times we think we will feel better if we don't talk about it and try to forget it. But this is a mistake. It won't go away. What should we do instead to start to feel better?

4. After someone we love dies, we might be afraid that others close to us will die or even that we might die. These fears are quite natural, but they can hurt us if we do not share them with someone we trust. That person can gently help us get over these fears.

5. Do you know of some Gospel stories or quotations and prayers that you could meditate to comfort you and to keep your trust in God alive? You might find some of these on pages 23 and 127.

HELPFUL HINTS FOR A BETTER LIFE

You are trying to become the best person you can be. Here are some suggestions to do just that. Read them one at a time, think about them for a while, and then try them!

1 ENJOY THE RIDE, NOT ONLY THE PRIZE!

Some people can think only about winning. They can't enjoy anything else. That's too bad because they miss a lot of fun that way. Here's some advice for you:

Don't always play to win.
Take the risk of trying new things.
Doing your best is all you need.
Having fun while you try
is what it's about!

2 CAN YOU PUT YOURSELF IN SOMEONE ELSE'S SHOES?

Some people never seem able to see the needs of the people around them. It's as if they are wearing a bandage on their eyes! But they are very aware of their own needs, as if they were looking at them through a magnifying glass! And they always take care of these needs first.

What about you? Are you aware of other people's needs? Do you appreciate other people's loving care for you? Decide then what you should do...

3 DON'T BE FOOLED

Advertisers always try to persuade us that we cannot be successful or happy if we don't buy their product. We know that's not true; they just want to sell their stuff. Don't let them fool you!

Of course we enjoy having new things. But we know they can't bring us to real happiness. Think about what brings you moments of true happiness.

Sometimes we fool ourselves by thinking that someone else's things are better than ours. Here is a short story about that.

Once there were two goats named Blacky and Snowy. Both were put in their own paddock, where they grazed happily. One day, they began looking over the fence and thinking: *It seems to me the grass is much greener on the other side. I would be much happier there!*

So Blacky and Snowy jumped over the fence and switched places.

But after a while, they realized it was all the same and that they felt better in their own place. So they switched back!

Whenever you feel like your life would be better if you had another kid's running shoes or jacket or rollerblades or whatever, remember Blacky and Snowy and don't be fooled!

4 DO YOU LIKE LIARS AND CHEATS?

Think for a while: How do you feel when someone lies to you or cheats you? Why do you feel that way?

Can you respect and trust people who lie and cheat? What if you happen to lie and cheat? How will you feel about yourself? How will others feel about you?

For example, during a test, if you copy from someone near you, you might get a better mark. But this won't help you learn. You are cheating yourself at the same time as you cheat others.

Lying and cheating destroy trust and respect among people. That's why God doesn't like us to do them.

Say yes when you mean yes and no when you mean no. (JAMES 5:12)

5 ARE YOU A GOOD FRIEND?

Good friends care about us for who we are,
not for what we have.

They don't gossip about us
and don't listen to others' gossip.

They stand up for us.
They don't lead us to do wrong.

Good friends bring out
the best in us. They look
out for us.

They have the honesty and
courage to tell us if they feel we
are harming ourselves or others.

They are able to work out their
disagreements and to make up again
after a fight. They are with us in hard
times and in happy times.

Real friendship is a wonderful gift we must look for,
treasure and nurture all our life long. Think about that
for a while and ask yourself two questions:

- Am I a good friend to others?

- What can I do to help my friendships to grow and
  to get stronger?

6 ARE YOU A PEACEMAKER?

This is how you can become one:

- Avoid gossiping or listening to gossip.

- When you feel that people are getting upset (in the playground, for instance), use your imagination and sense of humour to offer a solution to the problem.

- Be ready to do your part – even if it means giving up your turn, playing a different game, or something like that – to help keep or bring back the peace.

*Happy are the peacemakers;
they are truly children of God.*
(MATTHEW 5:9)

7 DON'T BE AFRAID OF YOUR FEARS!

We are all afraid of many things, even if we don't like others to know it. But there is no shame in that. It is quite natural.

- We might be afraid of not doing well in school or in sports, of losing the love of someone we care about a lot, of being bullied by older kids or even adults.

- We might be afraid of the dark, of heights, of dogs or anything else.

- We might be afraid of dying, or of someone we love getting sick or dying, or going away.

What should we do about our fears? The most important thing is to share them with someone we really trust.

When we share them, we feel better because we are not facing them alone anymore.

8 ARE YOU ABLE TO ADMIT YOUR MISTAKES?

Sometimes we do something wrong (on purpose or by accident). This happens to all of us. It is not a sign of weakness but a sign of honesty and courage to say: *It's my fault. I'm sorry.*

9 WHO DO YOU SPEND TIME WITH?

Jesus always looked out for the poor, the weak, the sick, and the people that others despised. He wanted to show them that he respected them and cared for them. He tried to help them whenever he could.

Who would Jesus go to first if he came to visit your school or neighbourhood?

What about you? Do you seek out mainly the kids who are the most popular or good at games, or well dressed, or have a lot of stuff to play with?

Or do you also look out for those who are often left out?

10 DO YOU KNOW THE SECRET CODE FOR POWER?

Too often our mind is like a whirlwind with a million things spinning around it.

Too often our heart is like a boat caught in a whirlpool of mixed feelings and emotions.

This often causes problems for us in our everyday life. When we feel this way we cannot concentrate and are not in control of ourselves.

Do you want to have more power over your body, your mind and your feelings? Try this secret code: **S.B.S.**, which stands for **Sit, Breathe, Smile.**

S.

- Sit down with your back straight. Put your hands in your lap. Close your eyes and calm down slowly.

B.

- When you are ready, start paying attention to your breathing. Breathe slowly, deeply. Feel each breath coming in and going out. Feel your chest filling with air, then letting it go.

S.

- When you start feeling quiet and peaceful, keeping your eyes closed let a slight smile come on your lips to relax your muscles. Continue breathing gently. Then silently repeat to yourself: *I am in control, all is well...* Enjoy the quiet as long as you feel like it.

If you do this often, you will be more in control of yourself. It will help you in many ways, like:

– to concentrate in school or on your homework or on prayer and meditation;

– to sort out your feelings, calm down when you are afraid or angry, and cheer yourself up when you feel sad;

– to be more attentive to those around you.

Try this new power for yourself and enjoy it!

11 DO YOU KNOW YOU HAVE A MAGIC WAND?

Your magic wand is the kindness in your heart and the smile on your face. If we want to, we have a million ways to light up little sparks of joy in the lives of the people we meet.

Here are some very simple ways to do that:

- smile at someone who seems sad,
- hold a door open for someone,
- give up your seat in a bus or your place in a line or at a game,
- share a snack,
- lend a helping hand,
- take the time to say a kind word in a friendly way: *Hello, How are you today? Please, Thank you, I like you, Take care, Well done, May I help you? You're great!*

Just try it and you will be amazed at how often in a day you can bring a smile to someone's face. You will also make God smile! That's the kind of world God wants us to build.

12 BE A SMART SURFER

If you are on the Internet, make sure you don't get hooked or just fool around with violent or silly video games.

Use it well. Look for web sites where you can enrich your mind while having fun and make new friends around the world.

13 HURRAY FOR KIDS!

Do you know what people who study our world tell us? Most often it is children who help their parents or other adults to see what we need to do to respect the environment, save water or energy, and care for the needy.

So hurray for kids! Keep it up!

14 KEEP LAUGHING!

Scientists have shown that having a good sense of humour is one of the best ways to keep healthy and happy. So keep laughing (*with* people, not *at* people) and enjoy your good health!

83

PART THREE

ENJOYABLE ACTIVITIES FOR THE WHOLE FAMILY

In our world today there are many different kinds of families. Some children live with both their parents, others with one parent. Some live with grandparents, aunts and uncles, or guardians. Some children live in two different homes and some have stepbrothers and stepsisters.

What the Lord Jesus asks of us is that whatever family or families we are part of, we learn to respect, understand and love one another more and more. One way of doing that is by sharing meaningful activities together. This part of your book will give you many ideas to do just that.

Don't be afraid to be the one who gets things started. Grown-ups often need children's fresh ideas and energy to get moving. So go ahead and enjoy life together!

If you are a small family, you might want to share some activities with other families you know. This would be fun for everyone.

TWO WAYS TO ENJOY YOUR FAMILY ALL YEAR LONG

1 A "WEEKLY SPECIAL"

Life is so busy, we often don't even have time to sit down together to talk. Sometimes our family table is like a cafeteria where we grab a sandwich or eat in a hurry to go out again. But that's not really what being a family is about, is it?

So why not decide together to give yourselves a "weekly special" like the Curran family did? This is how it might work.

At the start of the school year, once everybody knows their schedule, set aside one day a week for a special family meal for all to attend.

Each member of the family takes a turn choosing the menu and helping to prepare it. He or she also prays a prayer before the meal.

During the meal each person shares some stories: the best and worst moments of the past week, the fun and the pain. If there were disagreements or problems, they talk about them and settle them together. The plans and concerns of the next week are also shared so family life can be planned in the best possible way.

It is a wonderful time of sharing and fun in which everyone can feel the love and support of the others. The family might end the meal by praying the *Our Father*, holding hands around the table.

The Curran family enjoyed this "weekly special" so much that when the eldest daughter left for college, she asked for the family conversation to be taped and sent to her! Would you like to give it a try in your family?

2 A FAMILY NATURE DAY

The purpose of this activity is to offer the whole family a wonderful day-long opportunity:

– to relax: getting away from the phone, T.V., fax, computers and daily routines;

– to enjoy one another, having a leisurely time to talk and to share;

– to admire in all its details the beauty and exuberant life in nature;

– to rediscover the loving presence of God in the very enjoyment of our life.

HOW DO WE GET READY FOR THE NATURE DAY?

- Pick a day when everyone is free. Together choose a favourite place to go: a forest, a lake, a meadow, a mountain trail, a beach, etc. Prepare together a big basket of favourite picnic foods and drinks.

- Make sure you bring along for each person a small notebook made of one or two large sheets of paper folded in four, and a pencil or crayon. Don't forget to bring binoculars and magnifying glasses if you have some.

- Leave early in the morning. (Depending on the season, you might be able to watch the sun rise.) This is how the day might unfold.

- Once you have enjoyed the scenery together for a while, take your notebooks and explore alone or in pairs a different part of the place.

  Use all your senses: look closely, observe every little animal; touch and feel the soft or rough surface of trees, leaves, moss, etc; breathe in all the different smells and perfumes; listen to all the sounds; have an adult help you find a clean stream from which to drink.

- In your notebook write or draw everything you notice: trees, flowers, plants, all kinds of animals, insects, stones, moss, etc. Bring home with you what you can without spoiling the environment.

- At a set time, you all come back to your starting point and share your discoveries. At some point, perhaps after you have enjoyed your picnic, make sure you take at least 15 minutes to relax, to sit in silence: listen to all the sounds you hear, breathe in all the smells, feel the sun and breeze on your body, enjoy the quiet of nature.

Take a moment to pay attention to your breathing. Breathe slowly, deeply. Feel how you are part, with all the living creatures around you, of God's great creation. At this very moment God's love is giving life to all creatures! Speak with God in your heart, sharing your enjoyment of the world God has given us.

- At the end of the quiet time, come together again to pray, giving thanks to God for nature. You might sing a favourite hymn or make up a litany. This is how it might go: each person names one of the beautiful things he or she has enjoyed; all respond by saying or singing a few words of praise. For example:

- Blessed be God for squirrels that climb the trees so fast!

All: **Glory to you, God our Creator!**

- Blessed be God for the little beetles that hide in the grass!

All: **Glory to you, God our Creator!**

- On your way home, share your impressions of the day. Talk about how your family can help protect our beautiful planet Earth even more.

- Your family can enjoy a nature day a few times a year. One day in each season would be a great idea!

CELEBRATING THE SEASONS OF THE YEAR

In turning around the sun, our little planet Earth
carries us through four different seasons.

Seasons bring us new activities, but also some special tasks and chores. A great idea is to make those chores part of the fun of the new season by doing them together with a smile. It is much quicker and a lot more fun!

1 CELEBRATING FALL AND THE BEGINNING OF SCHOOL

Here are some ideas to enjoy fall in your family:

- When the time comes to clean up and put away summer clothes and sports gear, do it together and share the good memories of the summer. When all is done, take a moment to thank God for all these fun times.

- If you live in a place where the leaves turn beautiful colours, go out to a park or to the country to enjoy them. Pick as many as you can. Back home, dip the loveliest ones in a bowl of melted paraffin wax and decorate your home with them. Don't forget to put some in your prayer corner.

- If you live on a farm, enjoy and take part in the activities and celebrations of harvest time and/or sowing time. If you live in the city, try to go out into farm country to admire the work of the farmers or celebrate with them. Thank them for their work.

- When you have done your back-to-school shopping, take a moment in the evening to show your things to one another. Share your hopes and your fears and wish each other a good and happy school year.

  Remember that millions of children around the world would like to go to school and can't. You might like to end your exchange of ideas with a moment of prayer to offer the coming school year to God.

- On the first day of school, get off to a good start. Say a cheerful hello to the teachers and your old friends. Keep your eyes and heart open to notice the new kids and welcome them in a friendly way.

  Be especially aware of those who seem shy or alone, to help them feel at home.

- When apple season comes, make a trip to a "pick-your-own" apple farm or buy a big bag of new apples.

This one is the biggest!

Have fun eating them and helping prepare all kinds of goodies with them.

Bring some to a neighbour who is lonely or who can't go out easily.

I love apples!

- And, of course, make sure you take part in your family's traditions for Halloween, All Saints Day and Thanksgiving, or whatever other feasts are celebrated in your region.

This will be beautiful at Easter!

- Invite your family to share a bulb-planting activity in view of Easter time.

Buy your favourite spring bulbs. If you have a garden, plant them at the required depth. Cover them with dirt and dead leaves.

If you don't have a garden, plant them in one or two large clay pots. Cover them with potting soil. Put the pot in a cold, dark place. Water it, keeping the soil very lightly moist all through the winter. (You will bring them out of the dark on Ash Wednesday.)

After planting the bulbs, enjoy a good snack together. Share your thoughts about the wonders of nature silently preparing through fall and winter for a burst of new life in the spring. Praise together the God of life.

❷ CELEBRATING WINTER

Depending on the climate where you live, there may be special chores to do to prepare your home for winter weather and get ready special sports gear.

Do your part in good spirits, sharing memories of the past winter and your plans for this one. You have grown and can do more things this year!

Winter brings along shorter days. We usually spend more time at home indoors. Make sure this does not turn you into a couch potato, or a TV or video game addict. Instead discover the many activities you can enjoy this season on your own or with your family. Here are a few:

- Borrow new books from the public library and discover the joy of curling up in your favourite chair to read them.

- Or explore the Internet to learn more about your special hobby.

- Learn a new craft and let your talents grow.

- Play games together as a family.

- Winter evenings are a perfect time to invite your grandparents or other older adults in the neighbourhood for a good meal. After you eat, sit and listen to their stories of old times. This will be fun for them and for you.

- Prepare the Christmas decorations you will use soon. Get together to make the family's Christmas cards or write messages on those you have bought.

- Handmade gifts are the best gifts because they are something of yourself: your ideas, your time, your abilities, and your love are all there.

Why not prepare (in secret) handmade Christmas gifts for your family, your best friends, your teacher or catechist. Making gifts would keep you busy for many evenings. And what joy you will share when you give them out!

3 CELEBRATING SPRING

As we slowly move out of winter and start enjoying longer and warmer days, we feel the excitement of spring waking us up from our winter routines! New life is going to take over, but first we must do some spring cleaning.

• Why don't you suggest that your whole family get together to do it? It is so much more fun that way!

Don't throw out things too easily. Put aside anything the family doesn't need anymore. Later you can clean and fix these things and give them to people in need.

Make sure you recycle everything you can: paper, plastic, pop cans, juice bottles, etc.

94

- Then it will be time to clean the yard and prepare the garden, if you have one. If not, do some seeding and planting on a balcony or in window boxes. Offer to help an elderly neighbour with his or her yard or garden chores.

I'll water them every morning.

– Around Ash Wednesday, find an old cookie tin. Fill it half-full with potting soil. Plant grass seeds in the soil and water it lightly.

- You could start to prepare a lovely Easter basket for the centre of your Easter family table. This is how you might do it.

They need sunshine now.

– Bring out of their dark winter home the clay pots in which you planted bulbs in the fall. Put them near a window with the tin of grass.

Baya, look how beautiful it is!

Hurray for spring!

Over the next few weeks, take good care of them and watch the grass grow and the bulbs sprout. What a delight!

- As a family, bring a spring bouquet to someone who is lonely or unable to get out. Stay for a visit.

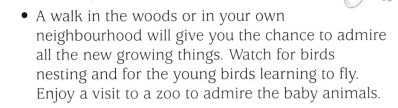

- A walk in the woods or in your own neighbourhood will give you the chance to admire all the new growing things. Watch for birds nesting and for the young birds learning to fly. Enjoy a visit to a zoo to admire the baby animals.

- If you can, plan a family trip to farm country to watch what is happening there.

- Decorate your prayer corner with signs of new life, such as eggshells, flowers and feathers. Praise God with love for all this beauty.

- Depending on your family traditions, you might start to prepare the Easter decorations you will display in your home or garden.

4 CELEBRATING SUMMER

At last, here comes summer and the longest holidays of the year! This can be for you a time to grow as a person and to enrich your life with new experiences.

The first basic change in your life is that you will have to organize your time. That sounds thrilling! During the first two weeks or so you can hardly find enough time to do all that you want.

But often, after that, parents start hearing: *I don't know what to do, I'm bored...* The secret to avoiding this boredom is to think at the start of the summer about all you want to do during your holidays. Decide which ones you want to do and then get started. Here are a few ideas.

• LEARN NEW SKILLS OR WORK ON YOUR HOBBIES

– Jason and his friend Graham often go into the forest with Mr. Peterson to observe the birds. They have even learned to recognize the songs of several birds.

– Sophie wants to be a botanist. With her little brother Tony, she collects flowers and plants, dries them and puts them in a large album. She looks them up in a botanical dictionary and sometimes on the Internet. She writes down all she learns in her book. Sophie and Tony love doing this and are very proud of their book.

– Joe and Anita like going to their grandpa's workshop. They help him and learn a lot. They are building bird houses for their garden and, in secret, are making a lovely bookshelf for their mom's cookbooks. They will give it to her for her birthday.

– Through e-mail, Joshua connects with Rajiv, a boy in India who loves to collect pictures of old cars from around the world. They share what they find and have a lot of fun and an amazing collection.

• DISCOVER THE JOY OF READING

Go and explore the public library. Ask the librarian for help in choosing your books. There are lots of good stories to enjoy. There are novels and also stories about heroes and saints of yesterday and today that you might like.

• USE YOUR IMAGINATION AND CREATIVITY

Sports are important, but keep some time for creative play. Make up your own games. Make up stories and prepare a show for families in the neighbourhood or for people in a nursing home.

• LOOK OUT FOR WAYS TO HELP

Tom and Valerie had a garage sale with neighbourhood families to raise some money. With their parents' help they used the money to organize a trip to the zoo for the homeless families of their town's shelter. It was a wonderful day!

• GIVE YOUR PARENTS A BREAK

Don't forget that your parents or the other adults who take care of you need a vacation, too. Do your part to make sure they get it. For instance, you can do some of the housework to give them a break.

Once in a while, you might surprise them like Krista and Jay did. With the parents of their best friends, they secretly planned a camping trip to their grandpa's farm. Their friends' parents would drive them there. All the children, including Krista and Jay's little brother Ned, would camp and help out at the farm for five days.

When all was arranged, Krista and Jay announced the good news to their parents at dinner with a pretty card that said:

Five days of holidays! Great!

> *FREE TIME FOR PARENTS!*
> *Friday to Wednesday.*
> *Enjoy yourselves!*
> *We Love You!*
> *Krista, Jay and Ned*

Let's enjoy their campfire!

• ENJOY SPENDING MORE TIME WITH GOD IN PRAYER

Because you have more free time, make sure you set some aside to pray, to meditate, to read books that can help you know Jesus better.

Invite close friends or your family to share with you some special prayer time. Use the first part of your book (pages 24-30) to be creative in your prayer life.

– Isabel and her best friend, Jackie, have chosen a special place in Judy's garden where they often go secretly. Judy brings a book about Jesus that she loves. They read a page or two, share their thoughts and meditate together. They enjoy that special time very much.

– Melissa, Patrick and their neighbourhood friends like having campfires in the summer. They do skits, tell stories, sing songs and always end with prayer and meditation. Everybody loves it. It has become a tradition to start and end their vacation time that way.

CELEBRATING THE CHURCH YEAR

Celebrating the major seasons in the Christian church year is an important part of following Jesus. Your parish religious education group or your school will help you to do just that. Here you will find a few ideas to celebrate these seasons with your family.

1 ADVENT

A) PRAYING FOR THE WORLD DURING ADVENT

Prepare an Advent wreath with pine branches or fir. Find a large ball or small balloon that can fit in the middle. Paint it blue. When it is dry, use bright colours to paint a simple map of the world on it.

You might hang it over the table from a lamp or the ceiling. Or you might put it in the middle of the wreath on a small plate so it does not roll. If you prefer, make a poster or place a globe close to the table.

Fix the four candles around the wreath. Set the wreath in the middle of the table. Whenever your family gathers for dinner, light the candle. (Light one candle the first week of Advent, two candles the second week, and so on.)

Then pray:

† *Dear God, you sent us your Son, Jesus,*
  to tell us about your love.
  You invite us to work with him
  for justice, reconciliation and peace
  on our beautiful planet Earth.
  We pray today especially for...
  (Mention here one country or part of the world you want to pray for and say why.)
  Please bless this food we are about to share
  and help us do our part to make a better world for all.
  Amen.

B) WOULD YOU LIKE TO BUILD A CHRISTMAS CRIB?

Begin during the first week of Advent and add to it during the following weeks. The baby Jesus should not be put in it before Christmas Eve.

- **The first week,** you might read with your family the Gospel of Saint Luke, chapter 1, verses 26 to 56. Then place Mary and Joseph in the crib and together make up a prayer to them.

- **The second week,** put the three kings on their way to the crib (but not in it yet), and fix the star over the crib. Share your thoughts about how God sends us people in our life to guide us to Jesus, like he sent the star to the kings.

- **The third week,** bring the kings closer to the crib and sing together "*O come, O come, Emmanuel*" or another Advent hymn. Now put the shepherds on their way to the crib.

Then plan with your family a special way of completing the crib on Christmas Eve.

For instance, you might gather around the crib. Read together the Nativity story in Luke's gospel, chapter 2, verses 1 to 21. Share the roles: one person is the narrator, others are the shepherds and the angels. You could sing *Gloria in excelsis Deo* or *Glory to God in the highest* during the reading.

At the right time, the youngest child brings the baby Jesus while another one brings a large, lit Christmas candle. Others place the shepherds and the kings around the crib. At the end of the reading, the candle-holder lifts the candle and says: *Lord Jesus, we believe you are the Light of the world!* All repeat the acclamation.

After a moment of silent prayer, you might end the ritual with a favourite Christmas carol and then wish one another a Merry Christmas.

2 CHRISTMAS

A) HOW TO SHARE THE JOY OF CHRISTMAS

Decide with your family what you want to do to share the love and joy of Christmas with others. Here are a few ideas.

- Get from your parish or social centre the name and address of a family in your neighbourhood that needs help because someone in the family is sick or doesn't have a job, or because the family has just arrived from another country.

  Go to visit this family, saying you would like to share the joy of the Christmas season with them and to learn about their own traditions.

- Remember you should always show others respect and care, and also help the other family see that they are making your own family life richer. When you get home from your visit, talk together about what you want to do next to help that family in other ways.

- You might also do this sharing with two or three lonely or older people in your neighbourhood. See how can you bring them a little joy and warmth at Christmas.

- If your parish does special projects like this, you could join them. What is important is that Christmas be a time of sharing.

The Johnsons have just met their new neighbours, the Kusacks, who have recently arrived from Central Europe. They invite the Kusacks to celebrate Christmas with them.

B) HOW ABOUT A SPECIAL GATHERING ON NEW YEAR'S EVE?

During Christmas week and New Year's, we are excited and busy. But it is important for a Christian family to find one quiet evening or afternoon to celebrate together in prayer the coming of the New Year. You might talk with your family about the following ideas and fit them into your own traditions.

PREPARATIONS

- At the beginning of the Christmas holidays, choose together the day and the time of the celebration. Find a large sheet of paper to make a poster; put it on a large table or tape it to a wall.

  Invite each member of the family to remember two or three of the most memorable, happy or funny events in your family's life during the past year. Ask them to note them on the poster with a few words, a drawing or a photo.

- Write on a small card this blessing, which comes from the Bible:

  May the light of the Lord shine upon you.

  May God bend over you with tenderness.

  May God bring you peace and bless you.

  Amen. (BOOK OF NUMBERS 6:22, 26)

- Ask your parents to give you the family calendars and date-books for the new year. Collect the ones from the year that is ending.

- On a small table in front of the family poster, set up the Christmas candle, the Bible, the little card with the blessing, a bouquet of flowers, and the old and new calendars.

CELEBRATION

- Gather the family. Light the Christmas candle and turn on all the Christmas lights.

- Start with a favourite Christmas carol. Sit down comfortably. With the help of the poster and of the old calendars, share your memories of the past year: the dreams, successes, failures, joys and sorrows, the "first times," the important moments.

- When you have finished, take time to pray. You might make up your own litany, with each person saying what she or he is most grateful for in the past year. The others respond: *We thank you, God of love.*

Then have one person say this prayer:

† **Lord, we thank you for the year that is ending.**
You know our joys, our sorrows, our hard times.
You know our plans and our dreams.
We know that you are always faithful
to our invitations,
always present at the centre of our lives.
Help us to make our family a place of listening,
of respect, love and mutual help,
and to make our house an open and welcoming home.
Amen.

- Next comes the central moment of the celebration. A parent or the adult who is responsible for the family says:
Let us now ask God's blessing on each other.

The parents bless each other and each child by placing a hand on the person's head or shoulder while saying the blessing that is written on the card. The children can bless the parents and each other if they want to.

- The parents offer each child a calendar for the new year. Then, while a child holds up the large candle, a parent says this prayer:

† **Lord our God,**
be with us each day of the new year.
Grant us health, peace, and happiness.
Keep us faithful to your love and close to one another.
May this joyous light bring us together again
throughout the year to share with you
our joys and sorrows.
Amen.

May the light of the Lord shine upon you.
May God bend over you with tenderness.
May God bring you peace and bless you.

Amen.

- If you want, talk about and write down on the new calendar some important events or special activities your family is looking forward to during the new year.

- It would be a great idea to end this celebration with the family meal or at least a snack together.

Happy New Year
to the whole family!

3 LENT AND EASTER SEASON

A) AN IMPORTANT QUESTION

Imagine that someone came up to you today and asked you: "What are you doing on this planet Earth? Why are you here? Will you stay here forever?" What would you answer?

Lent is a time when our Church is asking us to think about the answer Jesus gives us by his life and his teaching. To help us meditate on this answer, our Church offers us two rituals:

- **At the start of Lent, the minister of the church marks us on the forehead with ashes,** saying to us: "*Remember, you are dust and to dust you will return.*" This reminds us that we are not here forever, that one day our body will return to the earth.

- **At the end of Lent our Church presents us with the Easter candle,** a symbol of the Risen Lord. When we light our candle from the Easter candle, we are reminded that God will raise us up like God raised Jesus, for eternal life.

- In the meantime, what are we called to do? We are invited to work with the Spirit of Jesus to make God's dream come true: the dream of justice, love and peace for all.

B) A FEW ACTIVITIES FOR THE LENTEN SEASON

Here are some ideas to help you share a great Lenten and Easter journey with your family.

- Start right away. On Ash Wednesday, get working on planting spring bulbs and preparing your Easter basket (see pages 91 and 95 for how to do this).

That's what we are doing here! It is a wonderful adventure and also a great challenge.

Each year, if we take the Lenten season seriously, we have the opportunity to become stronger so we can meet this challenge and live that adventure. To help us do that, the Church invites us to a **personal conversion**. This means opening our heart even more to God's call and to the love of others.

One way to do that could be to give more time to prayer and to read a book about Jesus or a saint (instead of a comic book!) before you go to sleep.

- Or offer to help a local agency that takes care of people in need.

- Ask the people in your family if they would like to help you build a beautiful cross of love and joy during Lent. This is a way to say yes to the Church's invitation to open our hearts.

Make your cross with some light wood or heavy cardboard: Cut out small flowers from different colours of construction paper. Put them and some glue in a box near the cross.

Every time someone does something kind or forgiving during the day, he or she can glue a flower on the cross in the evening. By Easter the cross will have bloomed!

- Choose together a sharing project.

You could take part in your parish Lenten project or do something as a family. Here is an idea:

– Place a piggy-bank near the cross where everyone can put some money when they freely give up a treat, an extra item, or a trip to the mall or the movies during this Lent. At Easter bring the money to a group that helps hungry children.

- Don't miss the celebration of Reconciliation that your parish will probably invite you to during Lent, and make sure you take part in the Holy Week celebrations.

EASTER

- Prepare a **special prayer** for the family Easter meal.

  – Set the Easter basket in the centre of the table. In the middle of the basket keep a place to put a beautiful Easter candle. Decorate the basket as you wish.

  – Place the Lenten cross in the room. Near it put the flowering bulbs you had planted and the piggy-bank with your Lenten offerings.

  – This is how the prayer might go. When all are gathered around the table, you light the candle and lift it up while saying or singing: **Christ is risen, Alleluia!** All repeat the acclamation.

Christ is risen, Alleluia!

You put the candle in its place in the basket and sing a favourite Easter refrain.

One of the adults says this prayer:

† *Almighty and loving God,*
  we give you thanks and praise
  for raising your Son, Jesus,
  from the dead
  and for giving us the hope
  that you will raise us, too.
  Look with kindness on this family
  who has tried to grow in love
  through our Lenten journey.
  Bless this food which we are about to share
  and keep the Easter joy in our hearts
  throughout the season.
  Amen.

Enjoy your Easter meal!

4 PENTECOST

Easter time ends with Pentecost. On this feast day we celebrate one of the greatest gifts of God: the gift of the Spirit.

After Jesus returned to his Father, the disciples were afraid that they would be arrested too. They did not dare leave the house where they were staying.

But one day, while they were praying with Mary, the house was surrounded by a powerful wind! A crowd of people gathered around the house. The disciples received the Spirit of Jesus in their hearts. Right away, filled with new courage and joy, they went outside and started telling the crowd that Jesus had risen from the dead and was alive.

Later on, Peter, Paul and other disciples went out into the world to tell people about the Good News of Jesus. It was hard work, and dangerous sometimes, but the Spirit of God was with them, keeping their faith and courage strong.

Over the years, Christians gathered in small communities in their own homes to talk about Jesus, pray, share the Eucharist and help one another follow Jesus and be his witnesses. This is how the Church began.

In one way, each one of our families is a mini-Church, a "domestic" or home Church. When we gather in faith and love around our family table, the Risen Lord and his Spirit are with us, too. You might remember this on Pentecost day with a special prayer before your Sunday meal.

SPECIAL MEALTIME PRAYER

- Prepare a nice centrepiece for the Easter candle on the table.

- Take the candle in your hands. Have a parent light it and say the following prayer:

† *Come, Holy Spirit,*
  Spirit of light and of love.
  All: *Come, Holy Spirit.*

  Come, Holy Spirit,
  Spirit of wisdom and of peace.
  All: *Come, Holy Spirit.*

  Come, Holy Spirit,
  Spirit of strength and of courage.
  All: *Come, Holy Spirit.*

You place the Easter candle on the table. Your parent continues the prayer:

† *Lord Jesus,*
  may this candle remind us
  that whenever we gather around this table
  as a family to share our life and our food,
  you are there among us
  with your Spirit of love.
  Amen.

The parent extends his or her hand over the table to bless it and says:

† *And now, God our Father,*
  please bless this table and this family
  so we may become more and more
  a true sign of your love for those around us
  who need bread, respect and friendship.
  Amen.

CELEBRATING YOUR FAMILY LIFE

• WHY IS IT IMPORTANT TO DO THIS?

Because it brings us closer to one another. It fills us with new energy and joy to go about our daily life and work out our problems.

Children often have more ideas than adults about ways to celebrate. Don't be afraid to be the "cheerleader" in your family!

What is the recipe for family-life celebrations? It's not hard and it doesn't cost a lot. The ingredients are:

– imagination to find simple and new ways to show love and joy,

– taking time to be together,

– a sense of humour to have fun together,

– sharing good food and giving thanks to God.

• WHAT DO WE CELEBRATE?

Many occasions, big and small, deserve to be celebrated. There are ones like births and birthdays, baptisms and first communions, anniversaries, Mother's and Father's Days, graduations, and others.

We can celebrate special events, such as moving to a new home, welcoming back old friends or meeting new ones.

But many other events in our family life can be celebrated quite simply and joyfully in our very own way. All the "first times" deserve to be noticed, such as starting preschool, elementary school or high school, making it on a team, winning a contest, or finding a job.

The next few pages offer you ideas for three occasions:

– your birthday

– a family renewal day

– a special celebration for when the family needs peace and reconciliation.

1 YOUR BIRTHDAY

An important day is approaching for you: your birthday!
Some people might be secretly preparing a few surprises
for you...

It will be fun to be the star of the day! But your birthday
means much more than that. It can be a new beginning
in your life, an important step in your growing up. Here
is a way to help you live it to the full.

The day before your birthday, set aside a good chunk of
quiet time for a special birthday meditation.

Meditation

- Start with the breath of life prayer (this is explained
  on page 24). End it by thanking God, our loving
  Parent, for keeping you so full of life all year.

- Then have a heart-to-heart conversation with Jesus:

† *Lord Jesus, as you know,*
  it will be my birthday tomorrow.
  I will be ... (say your age) *years old!*
  With you I would like to go over
  the journey of my life
  since my last birthday...

– Talk to Jesus about your dreams that came true,
  the new friends you made, the things you did
  well at school, in sports and in other activities.

  Remember the happiest moments or days of
  the year, the love that was given to you, the
  ways you tried to live as a friend of Jesus and
  the joy this gave you. Then thank Jesus for all of
  that:

† *Lord Jesus, I thank you for all those sunny days.*
  Thank you for helping me to grow as a person
  and to discover the joy of becoming your friend
  more and more.

– Now talk to Jesus about the less happy times you had this year: problems at home or in school, failures, disappointments, your mistakes or things you did that were wrong. Show your trust in him:

† *Lord Jesus, even if I did not always think of it,*
I know you were always with me,
helping me through my hard times.
I know you have forgiven me
all my mistakes and things I did that were wrong.
I trust in your mercy.
Please help me grow in your love
and give me your peace
during this next year of my life.

– Now think about the coming year. Tell Jesus about your dreams and hopes. Tell him about your fears and worries. Ask him to guide you through the year:

† *Lord Jesus, let me ask you now*
to bless this coming year.
Please send me your Spirit
to guide me in your ways.
Please help me make my dreams come true
so I can become the best person I can be.
Lord Jesus, my true friend,
I know you will be with me
every day of this coming year.
I love you and trust you. Amen.

• If your family has a birthday party for you, it might be nice for you to make a thank-you for them: a poem, a song, a pretty card... Think of what they would enjoy most and do it.

And now,
Happy birthday to you!

2 FAMILY RENEWAL DAY

Family life is a very strange thing! Some days are wonderful. They are full of tender care, fun and joy. On these days, we love our family. We think it's the best in the world and would not want to be anywhere else! You have a good example of that on page 114.

Other days are terrible. They are so full of hassle, fighting and anger that we hate our family. We think it's the worst in the world and wish we could run away from it!

Everything is going wrong this week at the Martins' house!

Every family in its own way goes through these ups and downs. It is quite normal. But we all wish we could have more of the good times and less of the bad ones! One way to make this happen is to have a family renewal day once a year. The next few pages will give you a few ideas on how to do this. Choose what suits your family best.

• DECIDE ON THE DATE

Any time of the year is good. Some families might like to hold it during Lent, which is a time of renewal for the whole Church. But the end of the school year or the end of summer holidays before school starts can also be a good time.

• PREPARE THE POSTER

A few days ahead of the day, make a large poster to show these three ideas:

– What I like most about our family life.

– What I don't like about it.

– What I wish we would change or improve.

Under each drawing put a little box, a note pad and a pencil. Ask each member of the family to think about the three questions, to write down their ideas and put them in the boxes.

• THE FAMILY GATHERING

– When the day comes, you might all work together to make a nice lunch with some favourite dishes. An important part of the meal would be a large loaf of bread that can easily be broken into small pieces at the table. Homemade bread would be great, of course, if it's possible. And it smells so good!

– Prepare a welcoming and cheerful table with a bouquet of flowers and a large family candle.

– When all are gathered around the table, you light the candle while a parent says:

† *Lord Jesus, you said one day:*
"When two or three are gathered in my name,
I am there among them."
As a family, at this special time,
we joyfully welcome and celebrate
your loving presence among us.

All sit down. You take the bread in your hands while a parent says:

† *Lord Jesus, when we share the Bread of life*
at the eucharistic table, we grow closer
to you and to one another as a parish community.

As we now share this bread at our family table,
please give us your Spirit of love to help us
grow closer to you and to one another
day by day.
Amen.

– A parent then breaks the bread in small pieces and passes them around. All hold their piece in their hand without eating it till everyone is served. Then all hold up the piece of bread and say: *Thank you, God, for this bread.*
Enjoy!

– During the meal, open each of the three boxes. Read the notes out loud and talk about them.

– You might end the meal by sharing ideas on two questions:

• Should we change or add some home rules or ways of doing things so we have a happier family life?

• Are we doing enough as a family to build a better world? (Talk about the environment, support and care for friends and neighbours, work for justice and peace.)

– You might close the meal by holding hands around the table, praying the *Our Father*, or singing a hymn.

– When the meal is finished, all might help with the clean-up and then enjoy a favourite family activity for the rest of the afternoon or evening.

❸ PEACE AND RECONCILIATION CELEBRATION

Most families have times of turmoil when fighting and anger seem to take over for a few days. When things start to calm down, if everybody agrees to it, a peaceful prayer time might help bring the family back together. Here are some ideas.

- Prepare ahead of time a favourite family snack: homemade cake or cookies, hot chocolate or a cold drink. Set it aside.

- On a small table or large tray, place a big family candle and as many small candles as you need (one for each person). Fix them solidly (for instance, in a piece of modelling dough) around the large candle.

- Choose some peaceful background music.

- Gather the family in a comfortable, cosy place. Unplug the phones. Dim the lights.

- Invite everybody to sit in a circle around the candle. When all are settled, turn on very softly the background music. Light the large candle. All listen to the music in silence for one or two minutes, then the celebration begins.

Parent:

☩ *God of kindness and mercy, you know we have gone through difficult days in this family.*
Please bless us with the gift of your Spirit, as we gather here to make peace with ourselves and with one another.
We ask this through Jesus your Son, our Lord. Amen.

A child: *Come, Holy Spirit,*
Spirit of truth and wisdom.

All: **Come, Holy Spirit.**

A child: *Come, Holy Spirit,*
Spirit of love and peace.

All: **Come, Holy Spirit.**

Parent: *Let us listen to God's Word.*

A reading from Paul's first letter to the Corinthians:

Love is patient and kind; it is not jealous or conceited or proud; love is not ill-mannered or selfish or irritable; love does not keep a record of wrongs; love is not happy with evil, but is happy with the truth. Love never gives up; and its faith, hope, and patience never fail. (1 COR 13:4-7)

Be silent for a moment.

Parent: *In the light of God's Word let us now remember the past days...*

Then let us gently bring ourselves to say three words in our heart to the people with whom we had problems: "I am sorry," "I forgive you," "I love you."

Whenever we feel ready to say those words in our heart, we will light our candle.

When all have lit their candle, a parent says:
God is Love. God is Light. In God there is no darkness. When we love one another, our heart is in the light. We are one with God because God is Light, God is Love. (BASED ON JOHN 5 AND EPHESIANS 5)

A child: *Let us stand now.*

Parent extends hands over the circle:

May God grant us joy of heart, and may peace abound among us. (SIRACH 50:23)

All: **Amen.**

All join hands and sing a favourite refrain, then hug one another and share the snack.

119

PART FOUR

PRAYERS FOR DIFFERENT OCCASIONS

Like we do with our best friends, we can speak to the Lord with our everyday words, about anything we want. The Spirit of God is with us to guide our prayer.

But it is good also, especially when we pray together, to use words the Spirit has inspired to other people who share our faith.

TO GIVE THANKS

† *I praise you, my God, for your love is eternal.*
I give you thanks with all my heart.

Loving and bountiful God,
you created the universe
and all creatures that dwell in it.
You made us in your likeness.
You share with us your power.
You entrust the world to our care
and invite us to enjoy it.

I praise you, my God, for your love is eternal.
I give you thanks with all my heart.

You sent your Son, Jesus, to reveal to us your love.
He welcomed the children and cured the sick.
He freed us from sin and taught us your ways.
He gave us your Spirit to be with us always.

I praise you, my God, for your love is eternal.
I give you thanks with all my heart.

PRAISE TO THE LORD OF THE UNIVERSE

Among millions of stars God chose our planet Earth and gave it to us as our home.

Seen from outer space our planet Earth is blue, circled with white clouds. It is very beautiful! Its beauty invites us all to sing our praise to God.

† For the sun that gives life and fills
our heart with joy.
Praise to you, God almighty!

For the moon and the stars that
brighten up our nights.
Praise to you, God almighty!

For the coolness of water that gives
life and refreshes.
Praise to you, God almighty!

For the song of the wind and
the rain that nourishes the earth.
Praise to you, God almighty!

For the fish and the birds,
and all living creatures.
Praise to you, God almighty!

For life and friendship,
for love and happiness.
Praise to you, God almighty!

Continue the litany as you wish, then say
this closing prayer:

† God our Creator, you made the universe immense
and beautiful for our happiness.
I give you thanks for its wonders.
I adore you with all my heart,
for no one is like you in heaven or on earth.
To you praise and glory for ever and ever.
Amen.

FOR JUSTICE AND PEACE

Sometimes terrible things happen on our planet. Some are caused by nature, and some are caused by people. When you hear about these on television or see them in the newspaper, you might like to say one of these prayers with your family.

† **God our Creator and loving Parent,**
  you want our planet Earth to be a happy home
  for the whole human family.
  But you know, it is not like that right now.

  Please, God, help us make a better world for all.

  We pray for all those who are suffering:
  the sick, the poor, the hungry, the persecuted.

  Please, God, help us make a better world for all.

  We pray for those who have no work,
  no food, no friends, no home,
  for the victims of violence
  and for all those in need of our prayer.

  Please, God, help us make a better world for all.

† **Holy Spirit, you change our hearts**
  and enable us to love.
  Please change the hearts of all those
  who want war, who want to take away
  from others their freedom or their food.
  Strengthen those who suffer
  in their fight against oppression.
  Rekindle in the hearts of all people
  the longing for peace and justice,
  and the courage to build them. Amen.

If justice and peace are ever to spread around the world, it is up to each one of us to become peacemakers in our family, our school and our neighbourhood. This is what Saint Francis of Assisi's prayer is about.

† *Lord, make me an instrument of your peace.*
  Where there is hatred, let me sow love.
  Where there is injury, pardon;
  Where there is doubt, faith;
  Where there is despair, hope;
  Where there is darkness, light;
  Where there is sadness, joy.

WHEN I'M IN A BAD MOOD

† *Lord Jesus, I feel moody tonight.*
 There are days when everything
 seems to go wrong, like today.
 So I don't feel like saying much to you tonight,
 but I am still your friend and I love you.
 I will try to get to sleep fast
 so I can forget about this day.
 Please help me make a fresh start tomorrow.

WHEN I AM TEMPTED TO DO WRONG

† *Lord Jesus, you know me well*
 and you see what is going on in my heart.
 I feel like doing this, even though I know
 it is wrong. I am sure you understand me
 and want to help me.
 Please give me the courage to resist temptation.
 Let your Spirit rekindle in my heart
 the desire to do what is right, and give me
 wonderful ideas to help others do what is right, too.

WHEN I FEEL SAD

† *Lord Jesus, I am sad this evening*
 because... (tell him what happened).
 You, too, were sad sometimes
 because people did not want to listen to you,
 because they tried to hurt you.
 You were not able to make your dream
 come true, because even your friends
 let you down during your Passion.
 Please, Jesus, help me, make me strong.
 I know you are my friend
 and you are always with me.
 I trust in you. Amen.

TO PRAY TO MARY, THE MOTHER OF JESUS

In the Church we honour Mary as the Mother of God and our Mother. That is why we pray to her and know she will listen.

Mary's life was closely connected to Jesus' life. When we say the rosary we honour Mary. We remember with love and thanks the great mysteries of the life, death and resurrection of her son, Jesus.

• In the **joyful mysteries**, we share in Mary's wonder and joy when she gave birth to her son and watched him grow up in Nazareth.

When Mary went to visit her cousin Elizabeth before Jesus was born, she praised God with a beautiful prayer. We still like to say this prayer today:

† *My soul proclaims the greatness of the Lord,*
and my spirit finds joy in God my saviour,
for God has looked upon his servant in her lowliness;
all ages to come shall call me blessed.
God who is mighty has done great things for me,
holy is God's name! (LUKE 1:46-50)

• In the **sorrowful mysteries**, we share in Mary's deep pain and sadness as she watched Jesus suffer and die during his Passion.

• In the **glorious mysteries**, we share in Mary's incredible joy when she saw her son raised from the dead and finally joined him in God's glorious kingdom.

Many Christian artists have painted icons of our Blessed Mother. Each icon, in its own way, helps us penetrate the mysteries of Mary's life. Take a few moments to meditate while looking at this picture:

• The Blessed Mother seems a little sad. Maybe the artist was thinking of the sorrowful mysteries in Mary's life while painting her... Think about them too for a while.

• Notice the wonderful tenderness and trust we can feel there is between Jesus and his mother. It is with the same tenderness Mary is looking at you. Speak to her with trust, then end with this prayer:

† *Mary, Mother of Jesus,*
teach me to open my heart
to the Spirit of love
just as you did your whole life long.
Help me to walk with joy, like you did,
along the paths of God.
Amen.

FOR THE HOLIDAYS

† *Lord Jesus, holidays are wonderful!*
   We feel free each morning to plan our day as we wish.
   We have plenty of time to do the things we enjoy most.
   But I don't want to forget you, my best Friend.
   I will speak to you often in my heart.
   I will try to make the people around me happy,
   for I know this will please you.
   Teach me, Lord Jesus, not to forget anyone,
   for parents and grown-ups, too, need to rest and relax.
   Lord Jesus, I thank you for these happy days;
   help me make them enjoyable for everyone. Amen.

FOR MY FRIENDS

† *Lord Jesus, I love my friends.*
   We have so much fun together!
   Sometimes we have great ideas
   to help people in our neighbourhood
   or share our fun with others.
   But sometimes we also have bad ideas
   that can harm others or ourselves.
   Please help us throw out
   those bad ideas and find better ones
   that can help us and others have fun. Amen.

FOR AWARENESS OF GOD'S PRESENCE

† *Lord, open my eyes*
   that I may see your loving presence
   in the gentle arms that welcome me,
   in the loving smile that comforts me,
   in the kind words that encourage me.
   Lord, open my heart
   that I may feel your loving presence
   in the sparkling joy that sometimes
   awakens with me in the morning.
   Lord, open my heart that I may sense
   your loving presence in the quiet happiness
   that fills my heart when I do my best
   and try to love as Jesus did.
   Lord, open my eyes that I may enjoy
   your loving presence in the profound silence
   that sometimes overcomes me with heavenly peace.
   Lord, open my heart that I may discover
   your loving presence all around me
   in my daily life. Amen.

MEALTIME PRAYERS

We all know how important meals are in our family life. For one thing, the good and healthy food we eat gives us energy. But is it only to share food that we gather around the table? When we have a chance to relax and have fun, to share our stories of the day, to share our joys and concerns, to feel understood and encouraged, we leave the table feeling truly happy and comforted.

These meals are key moments in our family life. They make the bonds of love between us even stronger. They also give us time to renew our awareness of God's loving presence in our life and to give thanks for it.

That is why many Christian families like to pray for a short moment before sharing their meals. Jesus himself, when he shared a meal with family or friends, usually started with a blessing to give thanks to God.

Even if your family is not used to doing this, you might give them the idea to start doing it once in a while. Here are some prayers you could use, or you could make up your own prayer.

Mmm! That smells good!

FOR SUNDAYS

† *Dear God, our Father, we give you thanks for this day in which we remember the resurrection of your Son, Jesus. Bless this meal, which will renew our energies and help us be lovingly attentive to one another. Amen.*

FOR A SPECIAL OCCASION

† *God of all peoples, we are gathered here to celebrate...* (name the event). *We give you thanks for the friendship and joy that unite us today. We ask for your blessing on us all. Please keep our hearts open to the needs of others. Amen.*

FOR A FAMILY CELEBRATION

† *God of love, your tender care for us is gentle and steadfast like that of the best mom or dad. We give you thanks for the family life we enjoy. Please bless us and teach us to love one another as you love each one of us. Amen.*

FOR WEEKDAYS

† *Lord God, we give you thanks for this meal, which will renew our strength. Bless those who prepared it. Keep us united in your love and teach us to share our bread with those who do not have any. Amen.*

FOR TIMES OF SICKNESS AND DEATH

WHEN SOMEONE WE LOVE IS SICK

† *Lord Jesus, you know how much
I would like N...* (mention the name)
*to get better quickly.
In the meantime, please give him (or her)
courage and patience.
Help me see what I can do
to give him (or her) encouragement
and comfort.
Amen.*

WHEN SOMEONE WE LOVE DIES

† *God of kindness and mercy,
you created us so we could share
in your eternal life and happiness.
Please welcome into your house of light and joy
N...*(mention the name), *who has just left this world.
Amen.*

† *Lord Jesus, you cried
when your friend Lazarus died.
You understand our grief.
Please be with us in these hard times
and teach us how to help one another.
Give special comfort to X and Y...*
(mention the names),
*who are going to feel very lonely.
Help us all find comfort in the hope
that N... is now happy with you forever.
Amen.*

**Jesus says,
"I am the resurrection and the life.
Whoever believes in me,
even if he dies, will live."**
(JOHN 11:25)

127

TO PROFESS OUR FAITH WITHIN THE CHURCH

Our Christian faith is shared by millions of people around the world. It is good for us to express that faith every once in a while to be in communion with the whole Church. You can do this by praying the Creed we pray at Mass or with this prayer:

† **God our Father,**
through your love you created the universe
to share your life and your happiness.
You make us in your image
and adopt us as your children.
We give you thanks and we believe in you.

Lord Jesus Christ, Son of the Father,
you came to live among us.
You give us eternal life
through your own death and resurrection.
You are with us forever.

We give you thanks and we believe in you.

Holy Spirit of God,
you awaken love in our hearts
and teach us how to pray.
You gather us in the Church.

We give you thanks and we believe in you.

God our Father, Lord Jesus, Holy Spirit,
you are one in love,
you free us from evil and from death,
you invite us to share your life and eternal joy.

We give you thanks and we believe in you.

FOR MY FRIENDS
WHO DO NOT BELIEVE IN GOD

† *Lord Jesus, I have some friends*
who do not believe in you.
You know them by their name and you love them,
but they do not know it.
Knowing that you love me fills me with happiness.
But how I wish they would someday
learn about that love and be filled with happiness too.
Help me be for them, day by day,
a living sign of your love.
Amen.